Full City

Gentrification, Hope VI, and the end of Public Housing
Communities in San Francisco: 1970-2003

By Lorenzo A. Gomez

Full City

Gentrification, Hope VI, and the end of Public Housing Communities in San Francisco: 1970-2003

Printed in the United States of America

Table of Contents

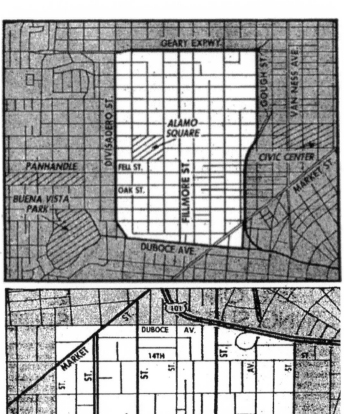

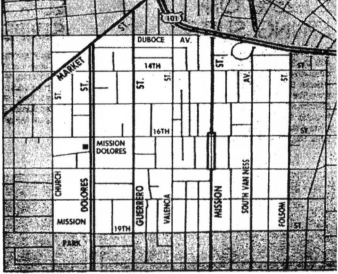

4

Prologue

The revitalization of San Francisco's subsidized housing communities under Hope VI has been implicit in the decrease of the city's overall African American, minority, and working-class population. Whether this was overtly the intention of city planners is debatable, the effects that this exodus would have on the process of gentrification were foreseeable. With the minority and low-income population greatly diminished in certain neighborhoods, many of the Bay Area's growing white collar or professional class felt comfortable buying property, making financial investments, and living in these areas. Interested parties of planners, politicians and investors could foretell the effect that the growth of Silicon Valley would have on the housing market; they were a generation in a line of planners whose intentions were to restructure housing in the Bay Area, seeing an opportunity to profit off the already tight market. San Francisco's first urban renewal project, the A-1 project begun in 1950, had displaced 4,000 people. Beginning in 1966, the A2 project further reduced the number of housing units in the Western Addition from 12,334 in 1960 to 10,306 in 1970. 60 percent of households were forced out of the Western Addition, and 15 percent were forced out of San Francisco. In this process, the SFRA (the San Francisco Relocation Agency, the agency which administered urban renewal in San Francisco) displaced 3,155 families as well as 3,984 single residents. The process of converting multifamily units and lodging houses resulting from the speculation and gentrification by private entrepreneurs which ensued, also accounted for a large percentage of this loss. The amount of affordable units built could at the most house a quarter of the population displaced, with the neighborhood having less than half of the units present when the A-1 project began in 1950. The last process of urban renewal, largely the subject of this book and taking place more through speculation and gentrification than through demolition, accelerated during Silicon Valley's renaissances in the 1970s and during the years in which the Hope VI plans were planned and implanted in the 1990s.

In 1994, after a five-year economic collapse, Silicon Valley's job base of 1.4 million began to grow, beginning with a 4,000-net job gain that year. This was a different boom than that which occurred in the late 1970's and early 1980's. While the first was driven by computer hardware, this one would be driven by the demand for semiconductor and software equipment to build high quality computer chips, a result of the global technology expansion occurring in the mid 1990's. For example, Lam Research, an equipment maker, doubled its income to $37.8 million in 1994 from $18.9 million only the year before. Applied Materials, another equipment maker, grew their income from $99.7 million to $213.7 million from 1993-1994. Both of these companies planned on hiring between 2,000 and 2,900 workers each in 1995. This economic boom would greatly affect the housing and real estate market of Silicon Valley. Of the 10 zip codes that showed the greatest home price appreciation in California during the first quarter of 1995, all were in Silicon Valley (with Mountain View having the strongest growth rate at 7.2 percent). As a result, workers began to look for other housing options in the greater Bay Area, especially in San Francisco.

The accelerated demand for housing for white collar workers resulted ultimately in the demolition of large, predominantly African American housing communities in an effort to gentrify the neighborhoods where they had been: Hayes Valley, the Geneva Towers, Buena Vista Plaza East, the

Bernal Dwellings, Valencia Gardens, and North Beach Place. When these projects were rebuilt, each was done so with fewer units and a diminished population of original residents returning to the rebuilt structures. After the rebuilding, only 48 percent of original families returned to Hayes Valley, 40 percent to Plaza East, 53 percent returned to the Bernal Dwellings, 36 percent to North Beach Place and only 17 percent returned to Valencia Gardens. This greatly reduced the African American population of San Francisco, and the gentrification that was expedited from this targeted removal further depleted the black and minority populations in these neighborhoods.

****

Chapter 1: Gentrification Begins in the Western Addition

The blueprint to redevelop San Francisco's public housing in the late 1990s can be traced to the redevelopment of Buena Vista Plaza West nearly 20 years earlier in the early 1980s. It is best to remember that the redevelopment process of the Western Addition goes back decades, taking place in almost two phases. The second phase began in the 1970s as speculators and investors began to try and take back neighborhoods with desirable housing which had become predominantly working class and minority, with government agencies such as the SFHA and HUD playing a role in the later stages of this second phase by minimizing the public housing communities in these neighborhoods and redeveloping them as "mixed use" under Hope VI.

Located on two blocks in-between Divisadero and Pierce Street, the original Buena Vista Plaza West (later renamed Robert Pitts Plaza) development consisted of three 10-floor towers bordered by walk-ups on Eddy and Turk St. Originally built in 1956 with a style embodying public housing built across the U.S. at the time, the SFHA partnered with two architectural firms, Community Design Collaborative and ED2 International, to modernize the buildings in 1982.

Tremors of what would ultimately be the displacement of this community and others over a decade later could be felt when the design team deemed all high-rise public housing as "...not suitable for families." In 1986, however, HUD's Comprehensive Improvement Assistance Program prevented the destruction and redevelopment of Plaza West because it did not allow for the creation of new units.

The design initially created by the two firms eliminated all semi-public and easily accessible hallway space. This design led to the reduction of only eight percent of units, but the public bid amount of $22million stalled the project from moving forward. However, when the SFHA design director began circulating plans of a rebuilt community that could be built for less money, the city granted the project $3 million, and the project was reborn. The implementation of this new design led to the destruction of 15 percent of the units, nearly twice the amount that the original design called for. The entire process, from the modernization designs begun in 1982, to its final reconstruction in 1991, took nearly 10 years. The redevelopments of other sites by Hope VI would come at a much quicker pace, after city managers had learned how to effectively deal with certain obstacles (such as resident opposition) and were able to see the impact that the reconstruction of Plaza West had on other variables, such as gentrification.

A common socio-political occurrence repeated throughout the history of the large or high-rise public housing communities that existed in San Francisco. This pattern consisted of these communities being condemned by the media and greater San Francisco society as places that were incompatible to the flourishing of healthy community/family life, with residents having to then defend themselves and their neighborhoods against these blatantly prejudicial depictions that were being used to further their communities' destruction and removal. One such instance was an investigative report conducted by a grand jury which depicted Yerba Buena Plaza West as being worse than a county jail. Many residents were outraged by the report, which used imagery and language based in the stereotypical depictions of inner city and public housing residents common at the time.

"I've been living here 20 years, and I refuse to accept (the grand jury's findings). Things just ain't as bad as they say it is." Said Lilian Philips, a resident in 1983 at the time of the report.

Phillips was one of many of Plaza West residents who joined members of the housing authority commission and staff at a press conference to rebut the report. Carl L. Williams, the executive director of the SFHA, said that it was very unfair to many residents for the report to characterize their environment using such sensational language. The investigators had explicitly written that conditions were worse than the San Bruno County Jail. Residents were incensed by this and other things wrote in the report.

"They come down here one day and try and tell us how we live, that we live in a jail. They should come and ask us," said Linda Williams, a 36-year-old resident who was quoted as saying at a press conference held in the laundry room of one of the buildings.

San Francisco Mayor Dianne Feinstein and other politicians condemned Yerba Buena Plaza West and Yerba Buena Annex in press reports throughout the 1980s. What had once been hailed as being a "paradise for the elderly" for the modern appliances and standards of living that contrasted with the single-room occupancy (SROs) hotels and tenements where the poor and elderly had lived before, were now being labeled as irredeemable slums by politicians and newspapers. When looking at the process of gentrification, as it spread from east to west and north to south minimizing the size of the Western Addition throughout the 1970s, one can see that by 1980 it officially ended on Divisadero Street, where Yerba

Buena Plaza West lay. Communities such as Plaza West were an impediment to further gentrification, and politicians and speculators used such loaded language in part to remove them.

It was in fact Mayor Feinstein who initially proposed converting Yerba Buena Annex into senior housing partly in response to several articles published in the San Francisco Examiner in June of 1981. Many residents who attended a housing authority meeting in August of 1981 to discuss Yerba Buena's conversion could see beyond the straw man arguments being used to mask the forced removal of the area's African American population.

"A lot of whites have recently moved into the community and they are down on project people," Said Benny Stewart, director of the Western Addition Project Area Committee. Stewart, like others, felt that it was part of a "'manifest destiny" attitude on the part of people moving in and renovating neighborhoods on the edge of the Western Addition."

Although the occupants of the converted Yerba Buena Annex were to be seniors, many of the seniors who were in the building prior to its conversion were not excited for its population change, as many in the elderly community were not readmitted because they had grandchildren or other family residing with them. One was Carrie King, a 95-year-old resident who lived in the building for twenty years since moving from Louisiana, where she had picked cotton for 50 cents a day. "I want to stay here and die here" she is quoted as saying.

Another was Virginia Herrerea, also a 20 year resident that had raised her family in the building, and who had let Governor Jerry Brown spend a night in her apartment as part of a well-publicized special report on conditions in the project during the 70s. "I don't want to move. I've been here too long. I've got my roots here".

Around 400 people lived in Yerba Buena Annex, including around a dozen elderly. Mayor Feinstein's plan of converting the building stood in contrast to the Housing Authorities plans to relocate the seniors and make it family only. Feinstein had written an open letter to the Housing Authority Commission, stating that seniors could be counted "to take their own safety seriously and to take every possible step to keep out those who don't belong in the housing project."

Carl Williams, then the executive director of the San Francisco Housing Authority, stood against this proposal and an earlier one by Feinstein for cooperative apartments to replace family housing in Yerba Buena Plaza Annex, stating he was "not aware of any place in the country where public housing has been turned into cooperatives,".

Despite Williams sentiments, Mayor Feinstein felt that the apartments could be sold to families that would maintain the properties. The Alamo Square Neighborhood Association, applauded Mayor Feinstein's proposal.

"The recent articles in The Examiner (The San Francisco Examiner had in June of 1981 written a series of sensational articles about Yerba Buena Annex) make clear to everyone the whole fallacy of this project as it is presently constituted," the association's president wrote the mayor.

Although only being given two weeks of training, weakly made billy clubs, and an existing vulnerable senior population to care for, security in the form of guards and other personnel were eliminated from Yerba Buena Plaza Annex in June of 1981 when President Reagan cut CETA funds.

Only with a contempt-of-court order did the San Francisco Housing Authority attempt to fix three major housing code violations just prior to the conversion. Despite these earlier cuts made to Yerba Buena Plaza Annex, 4.5 million dollars were available for new renovations, as well as 24-hour security, when Yerba Buena Annex was converted to senior only housing.

The staff of the housing authority's initial proposal was to lower the density of the 211 unit building by increasing the size of its apartments. This would be done by combining 60 one-bedroom units and 43 studios to create more two-bedroom units. Theoretically, by reducing the number of residents, the wear on services are reduced and the living quarters improved. The building would then become the home of more children and families bringing more stability to the community. However, despite the cost of this proposal being $3 million, it was set aside in favor of Mayor Feinstein's plan to convert the building to senior only occupants, despite the mayor's plan having a minimum estimated cost of $4.2 million. Although there was considerable support amongst the housing authority for the reduction plan, the mayor's advocacy of the all-elderly conversion made it almost certain that the authority's proposal would be rejected. Because of the failure and eventual demolition of Pruit Igoe in St. Louis, there was an orthodoxy of consensus amongst some influential municipal officials and politicians that high-rise public housing did not work. Feinstein's plan was similar to that undertaken in Philadelphia, where Wilson Park and King Plaza, two large public housing communities, were converted to senior only occupancy.

Other options considered at the meeting before the planning commission held on August 13th, 1981, were to close it, have it managed by tenants or by private capital, reducing the number of residents, or having its population become mixed income. Carl Williams, the executive director of the SFHA, did not feel that closing the building was an option with a waiting list of 7,000 applicants. Although not really contemplated for Yerba Buena Annex, a mixed income community model was already being considered by housing officials in 1981 for Yerba Buena Plaza East and West. Such a model for redeveloping public housing would be following those such as West Brighton and Stapleton in Staten Island, where 1,700 and 2,500 residents lived respectively. These communities had succeeded in bringing in many working-class families to live alongside those that were low income through an aggressive add campaign, and sending them in a more positive direction as communities. "That's exactly what we want to do to the plaza," said Williams, further noting that HUD had been asked for funds to help bring working class families to the two communities. Williams did not really consider private management as a good option stating that it would only be correct to do so if Yerba Buena Plaza Annex were in "an abandonment situation," which aligned with his perspective that "the Pink Palace does not come close to abandonment" in comparison to public housing in other cities.

The SFHA Commissioners, nearly all Feinstein appointees, voted unanimously in August of 1981 to convert Yerba Buena Annex from being housing for low-income families to housing only senior tenants.

The statements made by Benny Stewart reflect the awareness that many had of the ensuing gentrification spreading into the Western Addition. Much of it was encroaching from Pacific Heights, a neighborhood which was once included as part of the Western Addition lying north of Geary along Fillmore Street. During the urban renewal of the 1950s and 60s which had cleared the Fillmore of much of its original housing stock, the four blocks between Bush and Clay Street remained untouched. Too integrated to be considered either the Fillmore or Pacific Heights, in the years prior to their gentrification, they would come to exemplify the unique multiculturalism of the Bay Area. In the 1970s, household income in the neighborhood surged 272 percent, almost three times the national increase of 98 percent during the decade. New names began appearing for it—Baja Pacific Heights, Upper Fillmore, the New Fillmore—which by 1985 had only two black businesses (Leon's BBQ and Ruth Garland's Nail Gallery) in the area north of Pine Street where there had once been multiple. Some, such as Upper Fillmore, were perhaps a double entendre, but each had their own distinct political meaning. Multiple small businesses that had long been established were all gone by 1979. These included Del's Antiques, Delilia's Originals, Fonda's Shoe Repair, the Full Belly Deli, American Fencing, Myra's Cleaners, the Basket Works, the Terrarium, Drapery Associates, Minnies Can-Do Club, Sing Lee's Laundry, Marina Pet Store, Hillcrest Bar, the University Hide Away, Henry's Fish and Chips, Sanchez Family Restaurant and Delicatessen, Florence Somberg's Variety Store, and the California Free Market (which had existed for thirty years). Many of the rents in the neighborhood had been set on a square foot basis and did not include any rates for inflation. Real-estate firms, such as the Catalyst Financial Corporation, were then able to buy from landlords and remodel them when the neighborhood became desirable. Gentrification was incipient; one could still find a few Victorians in the area for under $300,000. Condos such as those at the intersection of Sutter Street and Fillmore Street were being built, for an asking price starting at $175,000. Down towards Geary Boulevard and the heart the Western Addition, one could still find apartments under $500. But the spreading gentrification and the building of new condos in different areas left city policy makers with an example of how housing that was in a minority area and previously deemed undesirable, held tremendous value and the potential for the exploitation of profit.

The black population of the 13 census tracts of the Western Addition decreased by 25 percent between 1960 and 1980 as part of the speculation and home overturn occurring during the period. Many investors were evidently aware of the impediment that the large public housing communities in the Western Addition presented to their financial goals.

"The Western Addition is not one homogenous area. I don't want to be misconstrued; what really matters in the Western Addition is proximity to the projects in terms of quality of life in the neighborhood. It has to do with the way The City runs the projects—the drug dealing, people getting robbed, the burglaries. I won't handle properties near the projects," said the owner of a property management firm in 1986.

Although the majority of the gentrification that occurred south of Geary Boulevard and east of Divisadero Street would occur in the 1990s after the Hope VI removal of Plaza East, the gentrification of Pacific Heights would lead to other areas in the Western Addition becoming gentrified as well. One of these areas was the stretch of Divisadero Street from Hayes Street to Geary Boulevard, termed Mid-Divisadero. In 1987 the majority of the corridors' stores and merchants were those such as A-One Hubcaps, Baptiste Fish House and Teresa's Hair Styling that catered to the area's predominant working-class African-American population. It was therefore a major event when local developer Samuel Chun built the Park-Fulton condos at the corner of Fulton and Divisadero streets. These condos, starting at $85,000 for a single bedroom, were less expensive than those being built at the same time in Pacific Heights.

The history of the condos built at this location captures a time in which residents were able to control the developments affecting their neighborhood in the early stages of gentrification. Prior to Chun's development, Windsor Financial (a development group from Los Angeles) had tried to install a chain of fast food outlets in the same location, but residents protested. They had realized the potential of their vetoing power, and as a result received through Chun's development amenities the neighborhood wanted—a grocery store, a hardware store, and other commercial shops in addition to 20 condominiums. This instance of peaceful, collaborative, resistance, contrast to others, such as when the Divisadero Heights Condominiums were burnt down in a $1.5 million arson fire in 1983.

The Fillmore Center

A major component to the gentrification of the Western Addition was the completion of the Fillmore Center. Speculators and investors alike on the fringes of the neighborhood looked forward to its completion. Years after the San Francisco Redevelopment Agency had removed black communities from and demolished 276 acres of the Western Addition, large sections of the neighborhood remained filled with undeveloped empty blocks. What had previously occupied the redeveloped space that would become the Fillmore Center was the Booker T. Washington Hotel, amongst 250 other businesses and institutions. Prior to the end of discrimination by downtown hotels, the Booker T. Washington had provided hospitality to such preeminent black celebrities as Joe Louis, Ralph Bunch, Sydney Portier, and Lena Horn. It also housed a popular bowling alley, Vernon Thorton's Bowling Alley. The story of Thorton's bowling alley is representative of the experience of other Fillmore businesses and their dealings with urban renewal of the area. When the process began in 1966, the SFRA did not purchase his business although it was in the targeted area for the planned shopping center. The agency rather demolished the surrounding housing, where most of Thorton's customers lived, forcing him out of business. He was then made an offer for a fraction of what his business had been worth.

The agency for decades could not find investors for the center, the largest obstacle being the inability to find a major retailer to provide a department store that would act as an "anchor" for a commercial development in the predominantly black neighborhood. There was also great hesitation from the private sector to build market rate housing, as well as internecine disputes within the redevelopment agency to build townhomes and other forms of subsidized housing that hindered the project from moving forward.

As a result, six entire city blocks consisting of 15 acres along Fillmore Street in the heart of the Western Addition remained abandoned; the exact four plots of this area where the Fillmore Center was eventually built would be abandoned for 20 years. Although this area running along Fillmore from Steiner Street to Geary and Webster Street to Divisadero, was the largest, it was only one of many within the area that remained vacant. When the Fillmore Center's construction finally began in 1987, it would be one of several condominium and apartment developments that would be built concurrently to fill in these lots. Others would include Cathedral Hill Plaza West at the southwest corner of Webster and Geary; the Winterland at Post and Steiner; the Amancio Ergina Village (which was the only development other than Tishman's to offer three-bedroom layouts) on Scott and O'Farrell; the Amelia on Fillmore between Bush Street and Sutter; Sutter Park West on Sutter Street between Steiner and Fillmore; and the Kimball Park Condominiums on Steiner street near Geary Boulevard. The earlier lack of enthusiasm for investment in inner cities on a local level mirrored that which was taking place on a national one; much of the San Francisco Redevelopment Agency's financial struggles could be blamed on the dismantling of federal programs under President Nixon for inner city neighborhoods renewed in the 1940s, 1950s, and 1960s. Part of the problem also was that cities (such as San Francisco) had become overzealous in their rush to remove poor and low income areas. From $38 million initially requested in federal funds for redevelopment, $109 million had been spent by 1975.

"Maybe San Francisco should have started with a smaller project area—it became overwhelming," said James Price, director of the U.S. Department of Urban Development in San Francisco during this time.

A tenant from one of 2,200 apartment units rebuilt in the Western Addition was more straightforward: "In a lot of ways, this neighborhood is a ghost town."

"This project will be the crown jewel of gentrification of the area," said the Sausalito based, Fillmore Center project developer Donald Tishman. To Tishman's credit, he did not view the Fillmore as a run-down ghetto, and he did not shy away from the project as many developers and investors had. He also initially hired three black developers for the project, and struck a deal with the housing authority to allow 50 percent of the construction workforce to be made up of local residents. When interviewed in 2018, Sonya Robinson, the president of the Robert Pitts Tenant Association, recalled that she had learned how to install dry-wall and other construction skills from partaking in the construction of the Fillmore Center.

For years prior to Tishman's project, rights to the land where the Fillmore Center was to be developed were held by the Pyramid Development Company. Its president was H. Welton Flynn, an African-American accountant and chairman appointee to then-San Francisco Mayor Joseph Alioto's public utilities commission. The board of this company also consisted of San Francisco 49ers players Gene Washington and Roland Lakes as co-developers. Even prior to this, Dr. Carlton Goodlet, an African-American physician and author, had led a group of seven developers (five black and two white), in the initiative to develop the land. Dr. Goodlet, who ended up being the inspirational force behind both the Kimball Park and Sutter Park West condominiums, was frustrated in his efforts for years to build condos in the Western Addition because of prejudice and restrictive practices such as redlining. In addition to a large department store, developers at this stage planned for the Fillmore Center to have a large cultural center in the middle, making it a cultural-heritage center similar to Japantown. Like the Peace Pagoda which presides over that complex, Justin Herman, the executive director of the redevelopment agency, and other development leaders, wanted a symbolic structure that would pay tribute to African-American culture. Like others involved in the project, Herman hoped that this retail and cultural center would help bring together, or be used by, both residents of the home-owning and predominantly white neighborhoods of west San Francisco, and black and minority residents from the Western Addition. Unfortunately, because of the Western Addition's status as minority and low-income, it never found the investors for any plans to come to fruition. Montgomery

Ward backed out of negotiations, following the national trend of locating major clothing retailers in the suburbs. Despite Tishman having developed projects in over 32 cities, no Bay Area banks would finance the project and he had to seek financing from Japanese, Canadian, New York and Atlanta banks. A 37,000 square-foot Safeway grocery store, still in existence, would ultimately be the cornerstone around which the Fillmore Center was eventually built. Although prior to the Fillmore Center the lots were not commercially developed, they were utilized as community spaces. Much of the land at the time of the Fillmore Center's construction was used as a community garden. It was also where the revived Juneteenth Festival was held for consecutive years in the late 70s.

Tishman's vision for the project was in contrast to the one many neighborhood residents and leaders had wanted, a small shopping center that would not have greatly affected the neighborhood's character, but would have provided a service to its residents. Neighborhood groups such as the Western Addition Project Area Committee, and neighborhood activists such as Arnold Townsend, imagined something like Clement Street that would restore the corridor to being the small business commercial district it had once been.

"Stop Tishman. Save the Fillmore. Wake up black people. Your community is being stolen from you."

This statement above was written on dozens of placards posted all over the Western Addition in 1986.

Beneath a picture of Malcolm X and Martin Luther King Jr. shaking hands, was an invitation to a meeting at the Ella Hill Hutch Center, dubbed as an 'eleventh hour' strategy session "to stop this white developer from taking over our community" and have the remainder of the Fillmore Center "built by and for black people."

Residents surrounding the development of the abandoned area that would become the Fillmore Center were not unanimously in favor of it or against it. A few long-term residents were able to invest and profit, and did not see Tishman's development as a negative change for the neighborhood. Lavonia Baker, an insurance broker, was able to buy three Victorians on Fillmore Street when the redevelopment agency had offered 10 for sale, for $200,000 a-piece, with each doubling in value by the time the Fillmore Center was to begin its construction. Baker would eventually own a 24-unit apartment building at McCallister and Gough, investing $1.3 million for its renovation in the 1980s.

"Sometimes when we talk about things happening in the Western Addition, we—blacks—just have to get in there and put our money where our mouths are. I know it's not always a rosy picture, but we have to do it." Baker said. "When there's change, there's always going to be people who are not able to conform to what's happening. With the cost of construction, you cannot rent apartments for $200 to $300 a month. Some people are going to be hurt. But there are great opportunities."

James San Jule, who developed the Amancio Ergina Village condominiums, was in general agreement.

"For one thing, its going to be better than a bunch of vacant land—better not only for the Western Addition but for the whole city. The people who make up those 1,100 units of housing are going to be people with good incomes, and the disposable income of those people is going to be focused on whatever commercial stuff is in the area. That's going to be a hell of a lot different than 14 acres that just produce cabbage."

Some local institutions also benefitted from the completion of the Fillmore Center. A key element in the redevelopment agency's decision to sell the land to Tishman rather than put it out for bid was his agreement to share the project with local blacks. The Third Baptist Church, which at the time of the Fillmore Center's construction was and had long been the largest black congregation in San Francisco, had a 1.45 percent share in the project and was guaranteed $300,000 for its prior attempt to develop the land. The church's agreement with Tishman was predicated on the development of 16,000 square feet of land to be developed into a convocation center that would potentially be used as the permanent residence for the NAACP and the African American Historical Society.

"The black community in this city is fragmented. There is no longer any sense of community, no social, cultural, or economic base. There is no place to say, 'Here is our platform, our place in the community', said Reverend Amos Brown of the Third Baptist Church in 1986.

Others concurred that Tishman's project was the final blow against the community maintaining a black identity. One was Gene Coleman, a member of the San Francisco City Planning Department at the time of the Fillmore Center's construction.

"The Western Addition is gone. On the whole, when there's construction and massive relocation, that's destructive. But the most destructive part is not moving people, its killing institutions: the churches, the bars, the guy at the corner store who gives you credit...There are some symbols of institutions in the Western Addition, but there are no institutional roots. You go looking for the community in the Western Addition and it isn't there. Someday, someone is going to study what happened in the Western Addition and write about it for the history books. It is too bad it will be its eulogy. "

Chapter 2: The Redevelopment of Plaza East and the Bernal Dwellings

It is important to examine the redevlopment of specific housing communities as they occurred under Hope VI in the 1990s of the several that were in San Francisco. Buena Vista Plaza East was a large public housing community consisting of two 13-story apartment towers and multiple three-story walk-ups. At the time it was demolished, its population was 97% African American. The towers were built in 1951 as part of the initial wave of "revitalization" which displaced thousands of families from the Western Addition who resided in the district's potentially valuable Victorian homes and buildings. Buena Vista Plaza East, together with other public housing communities that were often concentrated in these redeveloped zones, made up a core of housing structures that held a large percentage of the city's African American population.

The necessity of such housing structures cannot be understated. San Francisco has since the mid-1970s been an expensive, tight housing market. At the time when the Hope VI plans were initiated, San Francisco was one of the most closed housing markets in the country. From 1994 to 1997, San Francisco's vacancy rate was consistently less than half the national average for large metropolitan areas. By 1997, the last year of the relocation of Plaza East residents prior to its redevelopment, San Francisco had a *1.7* percent vacancy rate compared with a national vacancy rate of 7.5 percent. The United States Department of Housing and Urban Development (HUD) called for the creation of 131 units of off-site housing using mostly section 8 certificates. However, the plan for this was never completed and was subsequently dropped.

To appreciate the impact that the removal of these large public housing structures had on the gentrification process of the surrounding neighborhoods, one needs only to look at the demographics of the neighborhoods both before and after the structures were demolished and rebuilt. The Western Addition, due mainly to location among other reasons, had long been recognized by real estate agents and developers for its equity generating potential. From 1990-2000, the neighborhood's population increased by 26 percent, four-times the rate of growth in the entire city; yet, within the same decade the percentage of African American residents shrunk from about 60 percent of the neighborhood to 35 percent. This represented a 26 percent net decline in those 10 years, despite the growing neighborhood population. During the same period, the share of non-Hispanic, white residents rose sharply, from below 20 percent to 32 percent. Thus, the ensuing gentrification caused the area's population to increase exponentially while simultaneously causing its African American population to decrease.

With so many of the neighborhood's poorest uprooted and displaced, many potential investors who would have otherwise been hesitant to buy property had no qualms investing. San Francisco Housing Authority (SFHA) officials in the early 2000s pointed to the luxury condos selling for $500,000 across the street from the rebuilt Plaza East as an indication of how greatly the neighborhood had changed, with many disbelieving that these developments would have been successful without the redevelopment. Two other indications of the gentrification which occurred after Plaza East was redeveloped were the decrease in neighborhood vacancies, from 7.1 percent to 3.1 percent, and a 22 percent increase in housing units during this period. Even with both large housing towers vacant in 2000, the share of neighborhood rental units increased by 86.4 percent.

The neighborhood surrounding the Bernal Dwellings, a major housing project within the Mission District, also experienced demographic changes as a result of this public housing community's relocation. Located in between the Mission District and Bernal Heights on what was then Army Street (later renamed Caesar Chavez), the Bernal Dwellings always had a demographic difference with its surrounding neighborhood. In 2003 when the rebuilding of the community was completed, the residents of the neighborhood were predominately Hispanic (51 percent) or non-Hispanic white (39 percent), while a little more than one percent were black. The percentage of African American residents had dropped from close to six percent in 1990. In contrast, 65 percent of Bernal Dwellings residents were black and 26 percent were Hispanic or non-Hispanic white. As with the condos across the street from Plaza East, it could be strongly argued that the gentrification of the Mission District near the Bernal Dwellings would not have occurred without the rebuilding of the Bernal Dwellings. According to a 2002 Economic Research Associates study, the median sales prices of single-family homes had increased by 186 percent (from $206,000 to $589,500) in the surrounding neighborhood since 1993, including a 17 percent increase in the year in which the renewed projects were fully occupied. At the time the study was published, the sales prices of single-family homes in the Bernal Dwellings' neighborhood rose from 82 percent of the Bay Area median, to 112 percent of the median.

From 1990-2003 there was a 6 percent increase in the population and a decrease in the poverty rate from 25 to 15 percent. To contrast, the poverty rate in the Bernal neighborhood dropped by 10 percentage points compared to a 1.4 percentage point decrease in San Francisco as a whole, and the vacancy rate in the neighborhood decreased by more than half from 7.1 to 3.1 percent. Some would point to these changes as signs of improvement. Others would state that they were indications of gentrification in a neighborhood where a sizeable segment of the city's poorest residents had been removed in the guise of "revitalization." With the introduction of the Hope VI renewal, the nearby neighborhood south of Precita Park was described as one of the country's best to live-in in an article for Money Magazine. None of this would likely have been possible without the displacement of the area's poorest residents and the ensuing gentrification.

The timing of the SFHA's implementation was suspicious at best. In March 1996, the housing authority's board of commissioners and executive director resigned, coincidentally at the same time the HUD recovery team arrived. San Francisco also elected a new mayor during this period (which spanned only a few months). During this chaotic period and without the explicit approval from the city planning commission, the housing authority began to relocate tenants in March of 1996.

When the SFHA's permit application was finally presented to the city planning commission in January of 1997, most of the residents had already been relocated. The commission scolded the housing authority for displacing residents before they were given approval for their changes in the relocation plans, but caved in and approved when their fears about seeming politically incorrect were abated.

To be sure, the revitalization project was not met without opposition from the greater San Francisco community. Many schools were rightly concerned that black residents would be removed from their catchment areas and San Francisco in its entirety, because of the extreme scarcity in affordable housing. Many African-American congregations feared losing their parishioners. Willie Brown, the city's first

African American mayor whom black residents had strongly supported, was worried about losing connection to this base. Overall, many prominent leaders feared that this would be a permanent relocation, stemming from sentiments that went back to San Francisco's history of relocation under the masquerade of urban renewal decades earlier.

These institutions were therefore reacting to long-term demographic trends which threatened their continuance. San Francisco's African-American population had already been steadily and sharply declining, by roughly 30 percent between 1980 and 2000 (from 84,000 to 59,000 people) Families with children also declined during this period, by 5 percent. The diminished members of these institutions were therefore rightly apprehensive about redevelopment plans that reduced public housing units and caused residents, most of whom were black families with children, to relocate.

Overall, San Francisco's planning commission was reluctant to approve the plans, fearful of appearing to be voting against the wishes of public housing residents. Families who used Section 8 vouchers, which were 53 percent of the original households of Plaza East, were those affected most by San Francisco's tight real-estate market. As noted, HUD had initially asked for the creation of 131 units of off-site housing for the use of section 8 certificates, but the plan was ultimately dropped. The rapidly changing housing market also caused great hardship for the 31 percent who were trying to relocate to other public housing facilities, with the vacancy rate at the majority of San Francisco's public housing facilities below 1.5 percent.

"They're planning on running us out. No one's taking any consideration as to how many black men are going to get killed in that transition." Said Malik Rahim, who with a former Bernal Dwellings tenant, organized the Bernal Dwellings

29

tenants to refuse meeting with housing officials past the December 1995 deadline, and delayed the 50 Million awarded by the Department of Housing and Urban Development to demolish and rebuild Plaza East and the Bernal Dwellings for weeks in doing so.

On average, new residents had much higher earnings after the Hope VI renewals. Average income rose by over $5,000 at the Bernal Dwellings (from $10,537 to $15,546) and $4,000 in the Plaza East community (from $9,635 to $13,606) even after adjusting for inflation. There was a five-fold increase in the percentage of those who earned income at the Bernal Dwellings (from 10 to 56 percent), while the number at Plaza East increased nine-fold (from 7 to 63 percent).

A compromising alternative to gentrification, public housing closure, and urban renewal for longtime San Francisco residents was exemplified with the development of the St. Francis Square co-op. Built in 1963 with funds from the International Longshoremen and Warehouse Men Union and Pacific Maritime Association, the 298 units comprising it were constructed when the waterfront unions were internationally integral to the shipping industry, allowing for working class families to remain near the center of the city, despite its proximity to expensive condominiums on Laguna Street and Geary Boulevard. It was the first housing complex built to replace the 6.9 acres of Victorian housing destroyed in the Western Addition. Its connection and roots with the maritime union community led to its walkways being named after multi-masted vessels, like the Oceana Vance, Quick Step, and Bertie Minor. The co-op also became home to many A-list activist from the community, including ILWU Secretary/Treasurer Leroy King (a member of the Redevelopment Agency Commission for over ten years), people's advocates Tillie and

Jack Olson, actor Joe Stryker, Elaine Black Yoneda ("the Red Angel" of the 1934 West Coast Waterfront Strike), and Carl Yoneda.

It success has been hailed as an illustration of how urban housing problems in low income housing could be solved through democratic volunteer management and a well-planned application of federal funds.

"Each member has a vested interest, since we each hold a share of the property," said Dugal Mitchell, who had used the GI bill to purchase a home in St. Francis Square after he had been refused loans to purchase a home for his multiracial family in other San Francisco neighborhoods in the early 1960s.

The community requirements are that it remains demographically reflective of San Francisco in terms of race, head of household, and age, as well as a low maximum income. The maximum was low enough that by the early 1990s it actually priced out many union members, being $33,000 for a single person and $54,700 for a family of six.

"There are 298 families and 298 opinions here. That's the way democracy works," said Carol Cuneod, president of the St. Francis board of directors in 1993, when discussing the community's strategy for dealing with problems and potentially divisive issues.

Chapter 3: Neighbors in the Western Addition

In 1970, Mayor Joseph Alioto named a 30 person committee to begin the restoration of the Haight Ashbury. It was to be broken up into five subcommittees to address upgrading the business district, educational needs, law enforcement, and housing rehabilitation, amongst others. Much of the Haight became zoned R-4 (high density, multiple residential), including both sides of the panhandle from Stanyan Street to Broderick Street, and some of the homes surrounding Buena Vista Park; in total about 894 parcels of property. A down zoning petition was officially filed by Marry Mullins and Lurilla Harris, both property owners in the zoned areas. What they and many others felt was at stake was speculation which would allow one-and-two-bedroom units to fall into disrepair as a prerequisite to the construction of multiunit dwellings on the lots they then occupied. The petition was an effort to reduce speculative profiteering and encourage owner rehabilitation and occupancy. There was a real fear that redevelopment would push out middle and low income families from the Panhandle.

This may have true, but the property owners that supported this petition were against all "high-density" housing, or any "not keeping with the character of the neighborhood." Such phrasing, although perhaps intended to prevent damaging speculation and the construction of pricey high-rises, was also used to prevent the construction of affordable and public housing. Many felt that the decline of the Haight, was in large measure due to the redevelopment of the Western Addition, and the deterioration of the buildings that were caused by the influx of a counter-culture population and minorities afterwards:

"When The City destroyed Western Addition 1 and 2, the people there had no place to go. The Haight was not a low rent area, the is no such place in The City, but it had been a moderate rent area, and when the blacks were displaced, bulldozed out of the Western Addition, the natural move was to the West. Housing was older, they could afford it, many apartments were subdivided repeatedly. Then in addition to that we had the influx of the so-called flower children. And those two blows to the neighborhood damaged it almost beyond repair." He goes on to say "What has occurred now, has been a shaking off of those real body blows, a determination by the people up on the hill (above or north of Haight Street) as well as down in the flatlands, to make this neighborhood a viable place for all of us, not just one class, not just one color, just to preserve what it was before and what has survived and to organize it in such a way that it is a good place for everyone to live."

Whatever the motivation for downzoning, as well as the aversion to the then current state of the Haight Ashbury by some property owners and residents, on April 24th 1972, the measure was approved by the Board of Supervisors. The neighborhood would become increasingly expensive over the next decade. A study by a planned Savings and Loans in the Haight found that within the neighborhood between 1973 and 1976, there was a 29 percent drop in recipients of Aid to Families with Dependent Children, and a 48 percent decrease in local food stamp purchases. Correlated to this drop was a sharp spike in rents as well as home prices. In 1970, the average monthly rent for the entire Haight Ashbury was $131, 97% of the city mean. The average home price was $33,200, or 108 percent that of the city. By 1980, rents had more than doubled to $285 and were now 107 percent of the city average. Meanwhile, the average home price had risen to 144 percent of the city average, or $150,066. Between 1970 and 1980, the number of African Americans in the three census district comprising the Haight fell, from 6,658 (33.1 percent) to

3,394 (19.9 percent). This displacement was the most dramatic perhaps in the flatlands south of the Panhandle, in the area surrounding Haight Street, where in the census track between Waller and Oak the black population was reduced from 2,596 (41.5 percent) to 936 (18.9 percent).

"I think the very famous diversity is imperiled. Deterioration of housing is not the key problem; it's the increased cost. People with lower incomes, people on public assistance, older people on fixed incomes are being forced to move," said Calvin Welch, a community activist and member of the Haight Ashbury Neighborhood Council in 1975.

The trend would continue over the next decade. "If you bought ten years ago, you've tripled your money," said Betty Moss, owner of Far out Fabrics, a store then on Haight Street, in 1985.

The harmful private speculation that resulted in the exodus of African Americans from the Haight Ashbury occurring in the years after its downzoning in 1972, was substantial enough that by 1979 the Black Leadership Forum (then a prominent civil rights group in the Bay Area) held meetings to address it.

"Speculators are a problem all over the city, but the most intense activity seems to be in the Western Addition", said George Newkirk in 1979, then a former president of the organization. "We have statistics showing rent increases up to 300 percent in the last few years and substantial changes in the makeup of parts of the neighborhood (the Western Addition)." Newkirk then went on to estimate that up to 25 percent of the Western Addition's black residents had been replaced, mostly from the area within and surrounding the Haight Ashbury.

Wallace Stokes, then the president of the Black Leadership Forum, held similar sentiments:

"I think speculation can be stopped, be we need to take steps soon to protect black ownership or the wave of people returning to the inner-city may just sweep blacks aside. There are tools available, such as the creation of community development corporations which could help people buy and restore their homes with low-interest loans and technical assistance. All that keeps the center of the district stable are the public housing buildings there. Everywhere else, the pressure is still building."

Only one street (Page Street between Stanyan Street and Masonic Avenue) was still noted as having African American home ownership and residents by the mid-1980s. The few streets north of the Panhandle (running along its length and northwards until Fulton Street), however, would keep an African American presence until the mid-1990s.

Changes in the Haight Ashbury could be seen in its home ownership rates. In 1970, only 14 percent of homes in the Haight were owner occupied, yet within 7 years, this number went up to 54 percent. Dean Anderson, who staffed the 409 House, a community organization then at 409 Clayton Street, felt that speculation largely had led to the increase in the price of housing.

"What happened up until this year (1977) was pretty much speculation. It wasn't people buying homes to move into, it was speculators buying to hold for a few months and realize a profit. A lot of buildings have changed hands four or five times in the last few years out here. But that is slowing down now, because prices are getting so high. The market just can't bear a whole lot more."

By 1977, he felt that there were two Haights, the flatlands around the panhandle and the hill area deemed the upper Haight.

"The whole north of the Panhandle is still largely black, homeowners, families, people who've been there for years and haven't been forced to deal with rising rents that have gone on in other parts of the neighborhood"

The downzoning of the neighborhood to prevent high-rise development and speculation, had prevented the construction of high-rises but not speculation.

"Although it seems to have topped off, there's been outrageous property speculation, starting in 1973, 1974. Rents have gotten sky high- a three bedroom Victorian flat now goes for $500" said Anna Darden, president of the HANC said in 1977, going on to state that "The number of non-homeowning blacks and Asians has decreased greatly."

Bette Mosias, who for years worked at her family's store on Haight Street and was on the board of a savings and loan scheduled to open in the neighborhood, had a very objective opinion to the changes occurring:

"There's always been fights out here between two lifestyles. And I don't know how to define them…The Haight is not a utopia, its rough around the edges. But there isn't any other street I'd want to have a business on….(the people moving into the Haight) are the kids of the people who moved out to the suburbs. They grew up and are moving back to the city to see what they missed, and they missed a lot." According to Mosias, absentee landlordism by owners who had held property in the Haight since the 1906 earthquake had held it back, until these owners sold in the 1970s.

The loss of families in the Haight did have an effect on local institutions. The great loss in families and children in the years after 1970 caused the closure of Poly High, which was deemed surplus by the Board of Education. The Haight was also divided between its counter-culture population, and middle-class white-collar population over the issue of the Straight Theatre. Like the Winterland, another prominent venue in the Western Addition which had hosted some of the best live recordings of guitarist Jimi Hendrix, the Straight Theatre was eventually demolished.

Prior to its closure, Polytechnic High School was a predominantly black school. Opposition to its existence however, started earlier, during busing initiatives in the early 1970s. According to the members of the Poly Parent's Group, it was a maneuver by the School Board to prevent white students from being bused to a black neighborhood by closing the city's black schools. The closure of the school occurred in conjunction with plans for the closure of Benjamin Franklin and Pelton High School, two other predominantly black high schools.

The Winterland Ballroom, a mecca of 60s rock n' roll shows put on by Bill Graham, would eventually be demolished on December 31st, 1978. Around the time of its closure, many had different perspectives on its future. Some wanted to see it torn down and turned into housing, including City Planning Director Rai Okamoto, who took a progressive stance on housing. In response to questions about whether he felt housing was appropriate for the site, he responded:

"If you mean subsidized housing, yes. If you mean institutional housing, no. The area is coming back. I don't completely buy the argument that it's still hard to market sites there. And I'm feeling a little bit uneasy about so called gentrification. The low- and moderate-income folks are being outbid for housing." Okamoto felt that there was a duality to the changes happening in the Western Addition, and that although the neighborhood had become more attractive and structured, "(he) didn't want it so much that longtime residents can no longer afford to live there."

For some, however, the changes in the neighborhood and the impending removal of the Winterland created an atmosphere of earnest. Elizabeth Simpson in 1977 was the last black property owner on the block across from the Winterland, being the proprietor of an 8-unit apartment building. According to her, other black owners had either moved to Ingleside or Daly City because "...they got a good price and weren't interested in rehabilitating the buildings. The neighborhood is taking on a good atmosphere. It's a nice area and could be made much nicer. I still don't go out at night, but there isn't as much fear. It's quiet now. You can talk to the neighbors. I can live with that."

Another person who was enthusiastic about the changes in the neighborhood and the tear down of the Winterland was Father Francis Cassidy, a catholic priest at St. Dominic's nearby, where he had been baptized 51 years before. This was probably partly as a result of the necessity of having to clean up garbage outside of the parish Sunday mornings after concerts before his parishioners arrived.

"The Change in the neighborhood has been just fantastic. I spent six years in Mexico, from 1970 to 1975, and its like Rip Van Winkle. Somebody got out a paintbrush and that was contagious. Then the artist came in, with their shingles and multicolors. Each year it gets better."

Father Vincent Cavalli, the pastor of St. Dominic's also felt that the venue was "an eyesore."

"I'd like to see it torn down. It's such a waste of space, especially when so many people need housing, family housing. There's a nice spirit here, and that would improve, especially if we could get more housing, especially if we could get rid of that eyesore."

However, some wanted to see the concert hall used more for community purposes of existing residents rather than housing. Mary Rodgers, the chairwoman of WAPAC (the Western Addition Project Area Committee) wanted to see it converted into a recreation center for children and office spaces for community groups. She wanted the recreation center to act as a magnate for marginalized youth. She admitted however that there were obstacles preventing the building from becoming a center for Western Addition residents.

"We'd have to purchase it, the city won't. But there are federal funds available through community block grants."

However, she was not entirely opposed to housing either. "I'd like to see the building stay, but if they can put up housing that poor and working-class people can afford, that would be preferable. I visualize something for the youngsters, but they need a place to live first."

Many in the City felt that the increase in housing cost was attributable to different causes. Harvey Milk, the first openly gay city supervisor in the history of any large U.S. city, felt that the blame fell on downtown speculators.

"It's the big downtown interest that have really been responsible for speculation in San Francisco. They're the ones who got the Redevelopment Agency to tear down older housing and keep the City's housing supply low."

Despite the first no growth plan being so detrimental in the loss of the Haight Ashbury's African American population, another plan, called the Mt. Sutro Community Master Plan, was put forth in 1976. The plan barred the medical center and institutions such as USF and Lone Mountain and St. Mary's Hospital from constructing any new facilities. It also would establish a policy of preferential hiring to the underemployed or the unemployed in the majority white neighborhoods surrounding the colleges and hospitals.

However, many African Americans in the Haight were angered that they had not been involved in putting together the community plan. They also resented the halt in expansion of UCSF because the medical center had been a good employer of affirmative action and because of the increasing enrollment of minority students to the medical school.

"Because of the medical center, we now have health centers in areas of California where we never had them before," said Richard Scott, a self-employed dental educator commenting that since 1969 the UC medical center had seen a significant increase in minority enrollment.

Dr. Carlton Goodlet attacked the plan's policy of preferential hiring, adding also that it was harmful to restrict a facility that served everyone in the city at the behest of middle-class neighborhood groups.

"To give job preference to people living in the lilywhite Mt. Sutro area is madness," he said. "We have got to begin to think of San Francisco as a neighborhood," further adding that he could never approve of the plan because health care was too important to allow a single neighborhood to restrict this service.

Idaree Westbrook, who had led minority opposition to the plan at a Planning Commission meeting, argued against the notion of "the community" being defined as the area surrounding the hospitals and colleges, or whether that definition should be applied to the city as a whole. She also disagreed with the notion that residents of San Francisco were denied healthcare just because there wasn't a hospital in their immediate surroundings, citing the city's relatively small geographic area.

Louis Nelson of the Black Caucus of the Medical Center, reminded planners that when jobs are cut, minority employees are often the first to be terminated, ultimately concluding that the actual policies of the plan would be detrimental to many important institutions.

Medical students, minority community advocates, and health professionals proclaimed a victory when a compromise was ultimately reached. Despite the fact that the resolution passed called for state legislature "to review and evaluate the University's long range plans with a view to terminating proposed funding for all construction," minority leaders felt they had secured a victory through the work of Supervisor Terry Francois, whose amendment to the resolution barred two important projects from review request. These leaders felt that further construction of these projects, a new building for the School of Dentistry and a new 15 story wing of Moffitt Hospital, were victories because of the large amount of inexpensive and free healthcare provided by the Medical Center and because of the center's enlightened affirmative action policies in enrollment and hiring.

"All Third World people owe Terry a debt of gratitude," said Tony Wagner, an administrator at the Medical Center who helped minority leaders champion expansion, in expressing gratitude to Terry Francois.

The compromise was struck during a turbulent afternoon Board of Supervisors meeting on March 8th, 1976. The council chambers were filled with those supportive of the expansion, spilling out into the hallway where they listened to the proceedings over a loud-speaker. With frequent outburst from the supporters, Board President Quentin Kopp threatened a recess to maintain order. Despite an unsuccessful bid to delay the question for two weeks, a compromise was reached when Francois agreed that if the dental school and Moffitt were exempted he would support the resolution.

Idaree Westbrook, who initiated the struggle for medical center expansion, called Francois "a man who played a tremendous role in bringing the Board to compromise on behalf of Black and oppressed people," further saying that Francois should be recognized by the black community as the "Black Citizen of the Week."

The Ingleside District in southwest San Francisco, began to receive an entry of middle-class African Americans beginning in the 1940s, starting with the Oceanview neighborhood and moving northwest into Merced Heights. The district in some ways became San Francisco's middle-class black neighborhood, juxtaposing with the predominantly low-income demographics of Hunters Point and the Western Addition. The black population of the three census tracts composing Ingleside rose from 3.7 percent in 1950, to 38.2 percent in 1960. Peaking at 62 percent (11,171 residents) in 1970, this number would fall slightly over the decade to 61 percent by 1980 (10,894 residents). 11.6 percent of San Francisco's African American population lived in the Ingleside District in 1970, when the census population for African Americans in the city was at its highest (13.7 percent). This was much smaller compared to Hunters Point or the Western

Addition where 21.3 and 27.2 percent of the city's African American population lived. 3 out of 5 African Americans in San Francisco lived within one of these three districts in the 1970s.

In 1972, 9 of the 11 census tracts in the Western Addition had a black population of more than 40 percent, and in 4, African Americans were 7 out of 10 residents. More racially isolated and homogenous was Hunters Point where in all 8 tracts African Americans made up more than 50 percent of the population, and in 5, eight out of 10 residents were African American.

Beginning in the 1970s, many parts of the Western Addition suffered huge declines in their African American population and institutions, aside from those living in public housing and many of the AME congregations which remained. The western border of the neighborhood was minimized to an area encompassing just west of Divisadero Street by 1980 (except for the neighborhood north of the Panhandle). Buena Vista Plaza West lay along this western border, and speculators at the time were keen on spreading these gentrification efforts east of Divisadero Street into the neighborhood where this public housing community lay. They would get their chance in the mid and late 1990's, expedited by Hope VI.

The Alamo Square Association was founded in 1964 during the fight that year over the city's plan for the construction of a freeway which would have run through the Golden Gate Park Pandhandle. As a result of the neighborhood's resistance to and victory over the redevelopment efforts that were intended for it as part of the plan, an 18-block district surrounding Alamo Square was designated to be systematically rehabilitated using funds from a government program called FACE (Federally Assisted Code Enforcement). Beginning in 1969, this program provided low (3%) interest loans to owners to bring their properties up to building code standards. It also made available additional federal grants to neighborhoods for improvements such as planting trees and burying utility lines.

The creation of the FACE program greatly impacted Alamo Square becoming one of the first neighborhoods to regain the interest of middle-class buyers in San Francisco. However, in the early 1970s, it was still affected by inner-city social issues. In 1969, for example, the park received new lighting after two murders occurred there. Marvin Edwards, the president of the Alamo Square Association, described the park in 1972 as having become the staging ground for muggings, and with Willie Glover, another Alamo Square resident, he campaigned for and received more police patrols for the neighborhood. It was, however, a neighborhood of long-term residents who stuck around even through periods of struggle.

"I wouldn't abandon the neighborhood, I think it's the same all over." Said Edla Walter, who in 1972 had lived in the neighborhood since before World War Two despite its economic downtown afterwards.

Many of the Victorians bought by the first middle class buyers in the late 1960s and 70s had previously been turned into multi-unit apartment buildings. Gregoire Calegari, a CPA, for example, bought the home at 710 Steiner, an eight-unit dwelling which had been divided into six apartments, and reconverted it back into being a single occupancy home for him and his family. However, throughout the early 1970s, despite drawing the outside interest of families such as the Calegaris, the majority of the neighborhood's 4,000 residents had not been displaced and it remained predominantly (60 percent) African American. The stunning architecture of Alamo Square, amongst other factors, was what drew Peter Witmer, an architect who bought a home in the neighborhood and a major advocate of the FACE program, and other professionals to it. Amongst other impressive architectural examples in the neighborhood stands the former Czarist Russian Consulate at the north-west corner of the park. A heyday for gentrification existed in the United States from around 1975 until 1980, spurred by many factors such as the gas lines of 1973 and 1979, the explosion in a well-educated baby boom households, the inflation of suburban home prices, the migration of gays to more tolerant cities and neighborhoods, and a national change in perspective towards certain housing stock (Victorian housing became appreciated and desirable). The redevelopment of Alamo Square, would affect the other areas along to which it was proximate to. Frederick Douglass Plaza, built in 1902, was perhaps San Francisco's first planned community. In 1970, efforts to refurbish 132 units of the development began under the leadership of architect Beverly Willis (who was credited for much of Union Street's revival in the 1960s) and preservationist Jeremy Ets-Hokin.

Victorian architecture had fallen out of popularity after World War I, with Modern architecture taking its place as the favored style for the design of American homes. Prior to this, during the Gilded Age of the late 19th century, Americans had wanted to copy the architectural styles of Europe, in particular Victorian England. After the war, however, Americans began to desire progressive ideas in many fields, including architecture, and Victorian homes began to be seen as antiquated. Edward Hopper captured this fall from grace in his 1924 painting *House By the Railroad*, which depicted an abandoned Victorian home next to a railway. After the stock market crash of 1929, many were abandoned or turned into multiunit buildings. As many fell into disrepair and decay with their lack of wealthy or middle class residents, the legacy of Victorian architecture as symbolic of haunted structures would become cemented with the 1938 publication of the Adams Family in *The New Yorker* (the home was depicted in issue published in November of 1945), as well as other popular culture depictions which came later, such as the television show adaptation of the comic strip, and Alfred Hitchcock's 1960 film *Psycho*. It was not until the publication of such books as Elizabeth Pomada's *The Painted Ladies*, published in 1978, that Victorian architecture again became nationally popular.

During the late 1970s and early 1980s, as redevelopment hit the northern part of the Western Addition closest to Pacific Heights, a parallel form of displacement was occurring in the southernmost part of the neighborhood, just above the Castro District.

At the intersection of Haight and Fillmore streets, on the side of the historic Haight-Fillmore building is a plaque giving a interesting account of the history of the building and intersection, a portion of which reads:

> "....The building's new owner... was known for torching neighborhood crack houses, while driving a blue '57 Chevy station wagon with yellow and red flames painted down the sides....

This account may perhaps be an example of revisionist history, but it does shed some light on a chapter of the neighborhood's history long forgotten by most that pass by this plaque. Indeed, there were quite a few arsons in the neighborhood in the late 1970s, and looking back upon the housing war that took place at that time, their character is questionable.

During this period, this area of the Western Addition, known as Hayes Valley, in addition to the Inner Mission, was hit hard by arsons. In the 26 months prior to December 1976, there were 33 fires in Hayes Valley, and 40 in the Inner Mission area around the intersection of 16th Street and Valencia Street. In 1976 there were 12 fires in a six-month period on Ivy Street (in Hayes Valley) alone. While these fires were blazing, there was a mass exodus of blacks from the Lower Haight (then called either the Haight Fillmore and/or the Lower Fillmore). Between 1970 and 1980, 4,000 African Americans left the neighborhood. One property owner gave their perspective on the gentrification taking place in the Lower Haight in a 1979 interview:

"I'm down here because the property is cheap. I want to have money and can maximize my investment here. The architecture is lovely." He then adds, "Why the hell should this gem of a city be given over to welfare blacks. Put them in Idaho, or at least Oakland."

With what the landlord described as "something of a pioneering spirit", he bought seven apartment buildings and 10 storefronts in the Lower Haight. He then proceeded to cheaply evict of all of his tenants by shutting off the water and forcing the health department to condemn the property, describing the black families evicted as "gracious" and "passive." "They don't know what's happening to them," he said. "In the past, I bought tenants houses where the Cadillac sitting in the driveway could have paid the down payment. "

The down payment perhaps, but the four-unit building the landlord bought in 1963 for $32,000 would have been hard to finance for many. African Americans had early been denied such bank loans when they had tried to buy homes in this area of the Western Addition and in other predominantly black neighborhoods. Lipper did correctly predict, however, despite his inability to attract business to the Haight-Fillmore building at the time, that the building would someday be worth millions of dollars (he predicted it would someday be worth $3 million).

This landlord was not alone in the manner by which he invested in the Lower Haight. Some, such as Mathew Wilson, another investor, were at least somewhat reflective about their role in the neighborhood's population turnover and dispersal. At 24, he was the co-owner of Daddy's, a restaurant and gay hangout in the Lower Haight which served over 3,000 meals a month. Wilson's original idea for the restaurant was for one called "Mammy's," where an all-black staff in all white uniforms would attend to patrons.

"I used to be a speculator, but I was cured of all that," stated Wilson in the interview, when he said the overheated housing market cooled in 1977. "Before 1977, you could pick up anything, kick out the blacks and put in gays, unload it in three months and make $30,000. What do you think 'good tenants' means in the multiple listings books? It means the dirty work has been done. It's what I've, what everyone's done." He did, however to go on to reflectively say "but you sap the energy of the neighborhood, you take and you don't put back."

Other gay residents of the Lower Haight in 1979 also wanted an integrated future for the neighborhood. "I don't want to take over anything. I don't want black people to leave this neighborhood. I do want it cleaner and healthier," said Wade Myles, the proprietor of a flower shop in the Lower Haight. "It's time for gay and black and Chinese to live together somewhere, and I'd like this to be it. I'll be the faggot florist and somebody else can be the straight fern bar, and someone else can run the soul food joint."

Although there were genuine intentions by those such as Myles, a real housing war did erupt. Real estate agents spoke of "purging" neighborhoods of blacks, and some planners and black leaders estimated that by 1979, the black population of the Western Addition had been cut in half and that 70 percent of the remaining population lived only in public housing. Accounts in papers abound with stories of mass evictions of black tenants who were either single parents, the elderly or the sick.

Many of the newer residents developed a real hostility to the long residing black population. "If you take out everyone between the ages of 15 and 21, everything would be fine. People don't know how to take care of their kids," said an unnamed Lower Haight resident in 1982, who had recently moved to the neighborhood. Sentiments such as this would be echoed and perhaps were what produced greater legal battles in the dichotomized neighborhood more than 10 years later.

By 1980, the Fillmore's western border was defined as Divisadero by the mainstream media (although other areas such as near Westside Courts and north of the Pan Handle in reality were part of the greater Western Addition and retained a black community). The neighborhood's population was still over 60 percent black and would remain so throughout the 1980s. African Americans had opened businesses in the Lower Haight, Haight Ashbury, and greater Western Addition since the 1950s.

"The Haight Ashbury was just like the Haight Fillmore (Lower Haight) is now. No one wanted to go in there and start a business because there was nothing there. But we did," said Lucille Jackson, who worked at her family's business, Jackson and Sons Glass. The business, like many black entrepreneurial pursuits and business at the time, had recently lost its lease in a gentrifying area (the Haight Ashbury) and had relocated.

"I have to give the guys credit for bringing out the beauty in these old houses," said Ben Stewart, the assistant director of the Western Addition Project Area Committee, a group which monitored re-development. "But the truth is, no matter what we did to them, those old houses wouldn't have had the market value they now enjoy as long as the neighborhood remained black. Only whites with money, competing for the city's limited housing, could make their value jump sky high". Stewart said this when he was told that gay speculators had accused black businessmen of lacking the imagination to invest in the area and make it a symbol of cultural pride.

The businesses that had opened and were present on Lower Haight during this period were indeed diverse and dynamic. Fifteen new business opened within the immediate blocks near the intersection of Haight and Fillmore between 1980 and 1982. Whole Foods Company, the original proprietors of the namesake, was operated by two gay entrepreneurs and co-owners of the Fillmore Café located across the street, Robert Guarino and Harvey Reigle. The founders employed a payroll which was half black and carried health-food products as well as goods necessary to prepare African American dishes and cuisine. Goldielocks, Jackson and Sons Glass, Two Jacks, A Rose Is, Gardan of Edam, and more than a half dozen others, were some of the new shops that opened in the late 70s and early 80s, many of which were run by black families.

Black proprietorship had always been difficult to maintain in San Francisco. At the end of World War II, there were more than 500 businesses in the Western Addition. However, banks made it difficult if not impossible for blacks to even buy property that had degenerated due to absentee landlords. Urban renewal would later remove 3,155 families,

3,894 individuals, and level hundred of these businesses. Many of the remaining residents were then forced out in the 1970s when middle-class investors began buying property and evicting residents.

"Blacks feel like the new American Indian, shifted from one reservation to the other," said Wallace Stokes, director of the Black Leadership Forum, in 1979. However, he did remark that the social animosity which existed between blacks and gays in the Western Addition was somewhat farcical in its nature.

"It's too bad the community is forced to make an issue of gays when the real issue is housing."

As the surrounding neighborhoods began to gentrify, opposition to the existence of public housing, where the poorest and remaining black and minority population lived (and which could not be displaced by the private market) increased. Records of opposition to the city's maintenance of, and continued support for, public housing by middle class gentrifies and others investing in the neighborhoods surrounding the Bernal Dwellings, Hayes Valley, and Plaza West, amply exist.

In 1988 the Planning Association for Divisadero Street (PADS), which was made up of a number of neighborhood groups, sued the city of San Francisco in Superior Court in the pursuit of obtaining an injunction to prevent the rebuilding of Yerba Buena Plaza West. Among other claims made in the allegations were that the project would bring "increased noise, pollution, population density, traffic problems, and crime." It was to be the first public housing project built in San Francisco in 25 years. Despite the fact that it had been planned for six years and that the residents of Plaza West had already been removed with the promise that some would be able to return to a rebuilt community, the vote by the board of supervisors came dangerously close from preventing the project from moving forward, with four of the seven supervisors opposing its rebuild.

"I'm not going to vote for another project that's going to become a graffiti ridden ghetto," said San Francisco Supervisor John Molinari.

"Its going to be the same sociological problems," said Supervisor Tom Hsieh.

Many of the members of PADS were residents of the renovated Victorians surrounding the area of Plaza West. At the venue where the vote was held, opponents spoke for hours detailing their objections (such as the fear of their children being exposed to AIDS needles), many of which were rooted in prejudice. Despite San Francisco obtaining approximately 15.6 million in Federal Funds when resources from Washington D.C. were virtually non-existent, the group wanted Plaza West to be turned it into a cooperative because owners were "more likely to assume responsibility for their premises than tenants."

"Everyone wants low-cost housing as long as it's not next to them," said Mary Helen Rodgers, one of the Western Addition residents at the meeting supporting the rebuilding of Plaza West.

In the years after Plaza West had been closed, the three large high-rises that had comprised it, except for being the home for about 30 youthful squatters, sat abandoned. A magnet for drug dealing and other illegal activity, poetry and graffiti covered its walls. Used by a political theatre group called Contraband for a performance, and as a shelter for anarchists attending a convention in San Francisco, its ghostly hallways often sheltered many of the runaways and homeless that had been removed from the Civic Center.

On April 14, 1988, a total of 203 townhouse-style units were approved to replace the original Plaza West high-rises. In the courtroom that day, shouting matches broke out between supporters of the new housing, and members of neighborhood associations who opposed the reconstruction of low-income housing units. An environmental impact report (EIR) had been called for by members of the groups opposing the Plaza West rebuild, although it had not been called for the Fillmore Center. Many viewed this as a stalling tactic.

"I see this really as an attack on poor black people," said Naomi Gray, president of the Black Leadership Forum, who was present the day the town-homes were approved. "The neighborhood obviously feels there should be no affordable housing for the poor minorities of this city."

Eva Williams, President of the Plaza West Tenants Association, concurred this sentiment. "It makes me mad when white folks think they can run over negroes. That's not right. We was there before they got there, and we going to be there when they leave too."

Even at the demolition of the project, the tension was no less palpable. A delegation of protestors made up of various property owners and organized by PADS met and clashed with supporters. The earlier environmental objections had manifested into a lawsuit to block Yerba Buena Plaza West (to become Robert Pitts) from being rebuilt. Housing authority president, Lewis Lillian, and executive director David Gilmore gave speeches filled with combative metaphors to convey the struggle with which it took to get the project rebuilt. Lillian, unlike Gilmore, was rattled by the jeers from the protestors who were kept on the edges by police. A peace ensued briefly for a public meal that had been provided after the demolition commenced with a few taps of the wrecking ball on the side of one of the buildings on Scott Street. However, it abruptly ended when protestors clashed with the local residents who enthusiastically looked forward to the new housing. Protestors yelled that Mayor Art Agnos, who was present at the lunch and had given a brief speech, "was building a new slum." One woman yelled back at them "to go boost their property values somewhere else."

During the process of neighborhood turnover occurring throughout the 1970s and '80s, there were instances of collaboration between the newer buyers in these neighborhoods and the San Francisco Police Department. On November 2, 1977, largely at the behest of new property owners in the area, the police department sealed off the 500 block of Haight (between Steiner and Fillmore). More than 100 people, including children and infants, were removed from their homes and herded into the foyer of an abandoned movie theatre at 560 Haight Street (then the Gethsemane Church of God in Christ, later to be converted into a bar called the Peacock Lounge). Each person was methodically marched in front of a green van whose windows were covered in gauze, to be identified by several undercover officers located inside who had obtained warrants for heroin sales. Forty-nine people were arrested in total in the initial raid, with the police returning the following day to take into custody five more. The raid was "months in the planning," said Police Captain George Eimil. "And were going to keep going back out there until we get them all."

"There is simply no justification for a police cordon which sweeps innocent persons into a net and subjects each of them to the harassment and ignominy which the Fourth

Amendment is designed to prevent" said David Fishlow, then the executive director of the ACLU (the American Civil Liberties Union). Fishlow went on to further state that the police had acted with "unfettered discretion," stating that a "free society cannot tolerate such dragnet tactics."

By 1994, the Lower Haight had become a neighborhood with more than a dozen independent coffee houses. It still had yet to succeed in maintaining commerce on Haight Street between Fillmore and Webster, with five storefronts vacant on one block stretch and a high rental turnover rate. Used Rubber U.S.A., a Lower Haight landmark, could not maintain its San Francisco location. Some of the other stores that were closed down were tuned into coffee houses or bars.

"This place is becoming a coffee and bar hangout for the grunge kids with skateboards. They've got two dollars to spend, not 40," said Mandana MacPherson, co-owner of Used Rubber U.S.A.

Proprietors and others, however, looked forward to the tear down of Hayes Valley North and South, viewing it as the only, if not the most effective, measure to reduce crime in the neighborhood. San Francisco Police Chief Anthony Ribera, however, noted that crime was already down almost 25 percent in Hayes Valley for violent crimes, exceeding the citywide average drop of 15 percent.

The neighborhood named after Colonel Thomas Hayes, who owned a mansion that occupied the entire city block bordered by Van Ness, Grove, Franklin and Hayes, (and who among other things was historically noteworthy for being a second at the duel with free-soil U.S. Senator David Broderick and pro-slavery California Chief Justice David Terry), had in fact been in the process of gentrification since at least

1980, when the Louise M. Davies Symphony Hall was completed. Law firms had also been buying buildings adjacent to City Hall to convert into offices for sometime prior to this. With Gough, Franklin, Grove, and Hayes Streets as its borders, its first wave of gentrification would initially only span from the civic center to the 101 freeway on ramp that existed in the neighborhood until the 1989 Loma Prieta Earthquake. The Hayes Street Grill, currently a neighborhood institution, was among other businesses that opened during this time. Surviving the fire of 1906, the neighborhood had previously been low-income since at least the late 1930s.

"It's nice to see things prettied up, but not at such a price," said a San Francisco City Hall employee in 1980, who had been evicted from his studio apartment on Ivy Street which he had occupied for 10 years prior for $115 per month.

Many of the new merchants in the area were excited for the Opera Plaza Condominiums to be soon completed, as well as the 600-space parking garage at 330 Grove Street. The garage had just previously been at the center of political controversy, replacing the building which had housed the Pride Foundation. Four buildings (all owned by the San Francisco Redevelopment Agency) in total were razed, with 70 units of low-income housing lost as well on the stretch of Grove between Franklin and Gough.

"As long as poor and black people cannot find housing in Hillsborough, in Tiburon, in Piedmont, and in Concord, then the city has no obligation to provide parking for rich people in San Francisco," said Don Hesse, a staff member of the San Francisco Human Rights Commission at the time (1977), noting that many of those who would use the garage would be from the surrounding suburbs.

For retailers in Hayes Valley, the removal of the 101 Freeway north of Oak Street after the damage caused to it by the Loma Prieta Earthquake, allowed for it to expand the gentrification from this earlier period. The San Francisco Planning Department, in conjunction with its housing authority's demolition of Hayes Valley North and South, hoped to create 500 units of "affordable" units where the freeway had existed.

Already by 1993 it was already known by many low-income Hayes Valley residents that of the 290 families that would temporarily be moved, 170 would never return. It was especially known by tenants of the one-bedroom units, because the majority of the new development units—to be privately owned and operated—would be two bedrooms or more. Most did not know where they would relocate to, however.

"They said they'd relocate us, but will I have the same amount of space?..." Will I be relocated in a worse area than I am now?," wondered Tanzola Alexander, a tenant of one of the one bedroom units at the time.

"I want to stay close to my family—somewhere where I'm known. I just don't want to be in a new neighborhood all by myself." Said one elderly woman who had been a resident of Hayes Valley South on Haight Street for 11 years.

Chapter 4: United Communities

The roots of organizing in the Western Addition to slow displacement, largely began in the 1960s as a reaction to the A-2 renewal program. In 1963, the Congress of Racial Equality (CORE) and its allies established the Freedom House in the Western Addition to agitate against the plan. Though it fell apart due to opposition from the mayor's office and the SFRA, it organized a homeowners association and a tenants' union whose members actively fought against renewal. In 1965 and 1966, activist from the Black Students' Union at San Francisco State created the Western Addition based organization the Community Action Program to defend and counter against the existing and impending urban renewal. However, they were shut down by the mayor, and ensuing elections of conservative candidates on the local and national level in 1967 and 1968 ensured their further closer.

Though it had momentarily paused, organizing by Western Addition residents against renewal again began when a group of activist ministers, after attending in 1966 a conference held by Saul Alinsky, decided to create an organization modeled on the methods taught by Alinsky. Gathering together many of those who had collaborated with or had been a part of the Freedom House, the group soon became know as the Western Addition Community Organization (WACO).

In 1967, WACO began a heavy campaign against the SFRA. Amongst other measures it resorted to, it held large scale community meetings often attended by over 300 people, picketed the office of the SFRA, sat in front of bulldozers at demolition sites, and seized the stage at more than one public hearing.

This groups intentions were made clear by Hannibal Williams, a student at San Francisco State who would become an ordained minister and its chairman:

"We've been misrepresented by a lot of people who don't speak for us. I'm a humble man, but one thing I'm sure of, somewhere in federal law there must be something about self-determination. It's our right and were here to get. We're not begging or asking for anything. It's our right, and we want it."

WACO was perhaps the most successful in achieving the aims of its goal to halt displacement and increase the number of subsidized units when it enlisted public interest lawyers to sue the SFRA and obtained an injunction against HUD dispersing further federal funds until the SFRA created a relocation plan. On December 16, 1968 Federal Judge William Sweigert granted a restraining order in *WACO v. Romney*, in judgement stating that "there has been no compliance by the local agency with some of the provisions on temporary relocation as required by the federal government".

The judgment rendered was a major victory for residents of the Western Addition. For one, it incentivized Robert Herman (the head of the SFRA) to construct more subsidized housing units from the 569 units constructed by 1970, to 1,868 by 1971. Sponsorship of the many community based housing developments constructed increased in relation to this. It also allowed WACO and its legal council in the suit, the San Francisco Neighborhood Legal Assistance Foundation (SFNLAF), to oversee continued and future relocation as well as prevent involuntary displacement.

This generation of Western Addition activist achieved another victory in 1975 when mayor George Moscone, who had been elected with the broad support of progressive activist and neighborhood groups, appointed Hannibal Williams to a position on the SFRA board. Williams and his allies on the board "set the agency on its ear", (Moscone eventually replaced Williams perhaps because of this), making boldened moves, such as choosing Wilbur Hamilton, a former ILWU trade unionist, to head the agency. Under this leadership, the SFRA's main focus became the construction of subsidized housing by community sponsors.

Such organizations were not without internecine turmoil. WACO created the Western Addition Project Area Committee (WAPAC), which reviewed SFRA activities in the Western Addition. However Hannibal Williams, who served as the chairman for both organizations for a period of time, was accused of selling out the agency and forced to resign. Tensions came to a high when its offices were burned down by an arsonist and one of its staff members was killed. Despite these earlier conflicts, the staff members of WAPAC would go on to found the Fillmore Economic Development Corporation, which would conduct rehabilitation projects, and became involved in securing SFRA jobs.

Many veteran organizers with WACO and its contemporaries went on to positions in the housing authority, SFRA, and other institutions, giving contact to those in higher positions of power to the residents of the Western Addition. Hannibal Williams went on to become the minister of the New Liberation Presbyterian Church. After the resolution of its lawsuit, WACO became a supplier of food for low income Western Addition residents.

The organizing from this period had its shortcomings, however. Neighborhood housing sponsors tended to choose applicants who were not the most in need but rather the best tenants. What all of this organizing had done essentially was create a new layer of government. The institutionalization of community organization altered the relationship of neighborhood leaders and their followers. Rather than view neighborhood needs in political terms, they began to see them more pragmatically. The main goal became the securement of funding for programs such as CETA, rather than community control of development. This lack of control and change in incentive created a greater dependency on City Hall, as well as disunity amongst groups as they vide for resources from a scarce budget. Despite the weakening of community independence, Western Addition leaders were left with little alternative. By taking a pragmatic, program-oriented approach, the WACO leaders and others were able to increase their resources, become influential in city wide decisions, as well as keep some of their political vision with which they started in the 1960s.

However, despite its efforts, this generation of activism failed to prevent many developments that they had sought to impede. From 1973-1975, many community sponsored public housing projects were confronted with acute financial difficulty, being only compensated and salvaged by Section 8 leasing. 15 percent of these projects did not survive, and many of those that did became surrounded by neighborhoods greatly undergoing change through gentrification and speculation.

The Geneva Towers' two, 23-story high-rise buildings, were prominently visible over San Francisco's Visitacion Valley neighborhood for more than 33 years. Originally built in 1965 by the Eichler Corporation, a building company that created many other prominent structures in San Francisco, the towers were hailed as "the private industries' answer to the shortage of medium income, multi-racial housing." Financed by the federal government, permanent restrictions were put on income levels and rents for tenants. From the beginning, the development's success was hampered by financial burdens, starting with the bankruptcy of the Eichler Corporation shortly after the Geneva Towers were completed. A period of further financial uncertainty followed, with the development initially being sold to a mortgage company and later to a private investor from Southern California. It was during this later period that the Eichler/Geneva Towers began a period of decline, although it maintained its function as an important structure that housed the city's least wealthy and working poor.

In 1974, the Geneva Towers were a mix of working families and about 60 families receiving some form of government assistance. The majority of tenants were African American, and rent ranged from $180 per month for a two-bedroom apartment to $200 for a three-bedroom apartment. Although stylistically exemplary of modern architecture, by the mid-1970s many of the buildings were damaged from neglect, with 90 of the 576 total units vacant. It was during this time that the Geneva Towers Tenants Association, led by a 24-year-old Merrit College student and Geneva Towers resident named Marvin Dumas, began to protest the conditions of the building. A property manager named Eugene Burger had been hired to manage the Geneva Towers, but according to Dumas, Burger managed it more as a tax write off than as a housing facility, leading to the property's deteriorated state. With a neighborhood community organization called the All People's Coalition, the Geneva Tower Tenant Association picketed in-front of Burger's home in Mill Valley. When this proved insufficient, the coalition interrupted a property management class he taught at San Francisco City College. An ensuing high-minded discussion between Burger and Dumas led to Burger firmly agreeing to a meeting he had canceled a week prior.

The meeting would eventually be held in the Towers' community room on Sunnydale Avenue. Apart from maintenance improvements, the tenants and the neighborhood group advocated for a stop to rent increases for three years unless approved by the association. Although concessions were granted for the tenants' request to improve the elevators and security, Burger would not agree to end rent increases. Tenants also requested for the management to do something about the water which seeped into many apartments. To this concern, Burger cited the economic shortcomings of his company, responding that, "...if the job cost $90,000 as estimated, there is no way we can do it." He did, however, agree to the establishment of a collaboration that would see a $50 a month reduction to one unit per floor, in return for selected tenants then working to supervise the community. Perhaps the greatest victory won by the tenants and community action group was Burger's agreement to help finance a child care center within the Geneva Towers.

A year after the protests were initiated, Burger stood with representatives of the community action group and the tenants association, and joked, "I never thought we'd be standing here like this today....As a matter of fact, I never thought the building would be standing here." To this, many of the organizers in the room broke into laughter. Forgotten was his role as an arch villain and the target of the residents' animosity. The mood in the room was amicable as people conversed and interacted with servings of coffee and cookies, celebrating a year in which many long-awaited improvements had been made in the community. Although the Geneva Towers would eventually be demolished in 1998, this instance of tenant-community organization, which began in March of

1974, elucidates the ability of San Francisco's low-income housing residents to organize and advocate for themselves and their communities, and that there existed at times peaceful collaborations between public housing residents and property management.

In the years just prior to the implementation of Hope VI, the communities that existed in Plaza East and other public housing developments strove to improve despite San Francisco's financially crippled housing authority. In 1987, residents of Plaza East brought in Thomas Coleman, a city recreation worker, who saw potential in the disinvested community. Together, they began a pioneering recreation program located on the premises of the development. With more than 250 children under 12 located in the project, it had one of the highest concentrations of children in the city and was in desperate need of a recreation area. The collaboration with Coleman was the beginning of a push to open a day-care center and a health and community center for young mothers. A year later, in 1989, their efforts garnered fruition. The center would be the site of San Francisco's first health and welfare center located in a public housing project. It was a watershed moment in the city's housing, welfare, and drug policy. Residents could now visit doctors and nurses within a mere walk from their apartments. Not only were services for single mothers and their children available for the first time in an area where they were most needed, but residents also had greater control of those services provided. Organizers placed the center in an area of the courtyard between the towers where drug transactions had previously taken place, staffing it with youth outreach workers, public health nurses and social workers. It also served as the site of 24 different employment agencies and a police escort system for seniors. Linda Williams, Dorinda Jones, and Babs Dow, three tenant leaders, had fought for three years alongside Coleman to open the center. It turned out that Plaza East mothers were just like their PADS counterparts; the push for the center came about as a result of mothers' fears about their children's exposure to drugs.

Residents of the Bernal Dwellings also made strides to improve their community, which like those made by the residents of Plaza East, the Geneva Towers, and others demolished, were overlooked by the city and HUD officials in charge of Hope VI. Many became members of a greater effort known as the Organizing Project. Started in 1983, the project was an effort by members of the clergy, as well as labor and community organizers, to develop civil leadership in low-income communities.

In 1988, the residents of the Bernal Dwellings began to organize. Much of their plan was based on earlier organizing efforts conducted in the Valencia Gardens, where residents had wrestled a 21-point agreement from public officials. Their plan became the model for community organizing used by residents in Hunters View, Potrero Annex, and Woodside Gardens—other public housing communities also involved in the Organizing Project. Unique amongst those who were involved in the project, the residents of the Bernal Dwellings chose traffic safety as one of their most important issues, and had the intersection at 26th street (where basketball courts had been installed) shut down. Members of the project made improvements that were foundational yet pivotal: graffiti removal, garbage pick-up, a fence around the drug-free zone, and improvements and maintenance on such things as fire alarms, which were notably faulty. Like the residents of Plaza East, they also campaigned for a child and healthcare center.

Despite the efforts made by residents such as those involved in the Organizing Project and at Plaza East, San

Francisco's housing projects would often receive condemnation as forlorn communities in the media, especially in the years which predated Hope VI. Newspapers would run articles and stories portraying them as uninhabitable to validate their destruction. While depicted as communities of criminals, statistics show that those arrested in them were usually outsiders. Of those who were arrested at Plaza East, for example, 90 percent were outsiders, and seven percent were friends and relatives of actual residents—leaving actual residents to comprise only 3 percent of those arrested.

"This is a decent community even if were poor. I don't want them to make it financially impossible so I can't raise my kids here. I want to keep my ties to the community," said Rosie Cuadra, a resident of the Geneva Towers.

Hayes Valley resident Eugene Jenkins was more honest. "It's a conspiracy to take control of the inner city. To get black people out of here." According to him, most residents were unaware that the communities when rebuilt would be done so with fewer low-income units.

Many residents would have been justified in their indignation and suspicion. The housing authority, as mentioned, never completed its plan to create 131 units of off-site temporary housing for residents. It also botched the relocation process by failing to allocate security deposits on time to landlords for relocated tenants, find replacement housing in the private market, and prevent the vandalism of several apartments of residents who hadn't moved. Along with the struggle residents faced to find housing in one of the tightest markets in the United States was the fact that facilities were rebuilt with far fewer units, meaning that the renovation of the housing communities necessitated a relocation of a certain percentage of residents. Hayes Valley North, which originally had 294 units, was to be torn down and replaced with 100 fewer units. Bernal Dwellings and Plaza east were each rebuilt with 130 fewer units. Finding temporary housing was made even more difficult by the fact that so many low-income families had already been relocated when the Geneva Towers were razed.

"The white people would love to live here, I have to move across the water just to get a place. That's not right," said Tanya Loftin, a public housing resident at the time.

According to Kevin Marchman, the federal official overseeing the SFHA, which had been under investigation at the request of Mayor Willie Brown, residents had long been misled into believing that all residents would return once the communities were rebuilt. Of the 287 families displaced when the Geneva Towers were closed in 1995, only ten remained in Visitacion Valley by 1998. Less than half (131) would move back to Heritage Homes and other developments built to replace the towers more than five years after the buildings were shuttered. The Red Cross was brought in by the developers to oversee the relocation, and the entire process was deemed a mess by many involved. "If this was a priority [of the housing authority] to move people humanely, there would be resources available to do that," said Sharon Bailey, the program manager for Red Cross who supervised the relocation.

One of the problems with Hope VI's actions in completely removing as much public housing as it has is that, although the 1992 final report created by the National Commission on Severely Distressed Public Housing (essentially the origin of the Hope VI program) stated that only 6 percent of all public housing units fit into this category of severe distress, the obtuse definition of severely distressed public housing has made it difficult to assess whether Hope VI has been eliminating just these units or indiscriminately redeveloping. Perhaps most importantly to the role Hope VI has played in San Francisco, federal auditors in the mid-1990s found that the program chose public housing developments that were the most adaptable to higher income redevelopment---not those that were the most severely distressed. This would justify skepticism of Hope VI redevelopments of North Beach Place, Hayes Valley, Buena Vista Plaza East, and Valencia Gardens, all of which are public housing communities which proximate on or are within gentrifying neighborhoods or more affluent areas. Hope VI has also been criticized for trying to socially engineer a mixed income model for redevelopment, a model for which factual support demonstrating its superior effectiveness has never been established, and which contrarily basis its arguments in assumptions about low income families and their communities.

One writer has emphasized that what is unprecedented about the program is how it has transformed the nature of public housing into what she calls "regulated public environments," defining them as

"...real world places where poverty is both experienced and contained. They are quasi-private spaces, where private partners distribute and maintain resources supplied by the public sector. They shape the material conditions and opportunities available for recipients, but in exchange set specific behavioral expectations that reflect a larger set of public norms. They occupy a spatial distribution that responds to the needs of land markets within a specific urban context."

Perhaps most evident to this point is the San Francisco Housing Authority obtainment of a 55 million dollar tax credit, the largest in California History at the time, to renovate North Beach Place (a public housing community located within the Fisherman's Warf), while public housing that was in Visitacion

Valley and Hunters Point (areas less susceptible to gentrification), remained excluded for almost twenty years from any major renovation efforts.

Chapter 5: Gentrification and Transitions in the Mission, the Tenderloin, South of Market, and around the Bay A rea

A lot has been written thus far about the loss of African Americans from San Francisco during processes of urban renewal and gentrification, but the Latino community also endured a dramatic drop in population, especially in the 1970s, when it fell by 17 percent. During this decade, the neighborhood which constituted the greater Mission was pushed eastward from Castro Street to Dolores Street, and the Latino population of the entire Noe Valley south and west of the Castro Neighborhood fell below 25 percent by 1980. It is important to note that the Castro, prior to its rebirth as a gay neighborhood in the 1970s, was an Irish Catholic neighborhood whose Latino population, despite its proximity to Latino communities, was always under 25 percent.

One of the first areas in the Mission to receive attention from outside investment was the area which historically had been the most densely populated, lowest income, and inhabited by the most recent immigrants—the upper Mission. In the early 1980s, when this began to occur, those involved called the area "the North Mission." The neighborhood still housed over 15 local unions, a testament to its working-class population (in the early twentieth century, after the 1906 fire, the area was planned as such when much of it was destroyed and redesigned as a blue-collar Irish immigrant/Irish American neighborhood). Perhaps the earliest indication of the neighborhood's shift was a 1979 loan program that was intended to help property owners and merchants on 16th street make improvements. The area had been hit hard by arsonists; from 1974-1976 there were 15 proven cases. Despite the good intentions of the program, it failed when the merchants could not meet the stringent loan requirements.

In the late 1970s and early 1980s the area became a center for lesbians and feminist. With businesses such as the Old Wives Tales bookstore, Amelia's Bar (a lesbian bar which paid homage to Amelia Earhart), Garbo's Hair Salon and Penny Lane (two barbershops owned and operated by women), and the Osento Women's Bathhouse, the neighborhood along the six blocks of Valencia Street between 16th Street and 22nd Street became known as "the Women's District" Other significant cultural organizations along this section of Valencia Street included the newsroom of the lesbian paper Coming Up, the Women's Information Exchange (law offices), and nearby on 22nd street the first Good Vibrations shop (a female oriented adult store started by feminist Joani Blank) In March of 1979, the umbrella organization the San Francisco Women's Centers made a down payment to buy the Dovre Hall from the Sons of Norway and begin its transformation into the Women's Center. Marya Grambs had raised money for the building since 1977, and proceeds to purchase it had come from a variety of fundraising events and sources. At the time it was purchased, only 20 percent of the building was being used, primarily as a hall where workers could socialize, eat and drink (there was a bar called the Dovre Club on the second floor which remained after it was purchased by the Women's Centers). Although it became a center for women's organizations, the original board of directors wanted to keep the building open to the Mission community, providing it as a space for the 1980 Mr. Golden West and Mr. Teenage Golden West Bodybuilding Championships, neighborhood youth dances, and other events. Two years after its opening, 13 women's groups, including the National Organization for Women, Women Against Violence and Pornography and the Third World Women's Alliance, operated alongside businesses that had been in the location for 50 years.

Also renovated was the Victoria Theatre, once a burlesque house, by Roberto and Anita Correo, becoming the home of the Theatre Guild of San Francisco. Many San Francisco art troupes relocated to the "North Mission" during the late 70s and early 80s, including the Oberlin Dance Collective, the Margaret Jenkins Dance Studio, Theatre Flamenco of San Francisco and the Ethnic Dance Center. The Roxy Theatre was also renovated during this period from being the pornographic theatre it had been the decade prior. The neighborhood in the early 1980s is often described as one being full of children playing in small streets lined with community gardens and family plots to get away from the busy intersections such as 16th and Mission Street. Youngsters boxed at the armory at 14th and Mission Street. All this began to change, and like the fate of the youth center and gym located there (the state put the armory up for auction in April 1982), the future of the neighborhood as being one for lower and working-class families became uncertain. At 15th and Guerro Street, 148 condos went up at the site of a former Foremost-McKesson dairy, their starting prices being far too high to be affordable to local residents. As families moved out, or were evicted, it became less common for other families to replace them. Prices for a one-bedroom apartment were already between $400 and $550 a month according to some estimates by the early 80s.

A few years earlier things had begun to escalate to higher levels between the Mission's older Latino population and its newer residents. In the late 1970s, graffiti began to appear along walls in the Mission, such as "Es mi barrio!/ Its my ghetto!"; "Stop Gay White Racism"; protesting the increased housing cost and the displacement it caused. The 1977 election for the San Francisco Board of Supervisors for District 6 (the district which contains the Mission) was a microcosm of the greater tensions felt between the two communities. Against Gary Borvice, the frontrunning Latino candidate and founder of the Mission community organization La Raza En Acion Local, ran Carol Ruth Silver. Silver, the candidate supported by most of the gay community, won, and Latinos were forced to recognize the political clout gays had in a district that many had felt was theirs. Throughout the election, Silver attacked Borvice for being "anti-gay", a charge which originated from Borvice's lead in a community movement to stop a lesbian bar from opening on 24th and Van Ness Avenue, and from La Raza prior being the only San Francisco group to oppose the decriminalization of gay sexual acts. Borvice attempted to mend the rift, and was actually endorsed by several gay community leaders. However, earlier in the year, the schism had already been deepened between communities with the violent murder of Robert Hillsborough, who had been attacked with his boyfriend after eating at Whiz Burger, then stabbed and beaten to death outside their home on 19th Street by a group of youths from San Francisco, San Bruno, and Daily City. A record breaking 300,000 people had shown up for the Pride March four days later, held for the first time on Market Street.

Over the next two decades, Dolores Park became a site of cultural encounter and sometimes conflict between Mission residents. In 1980, many were again shaken when three Mission youths were charged with assaulting two men, one of whom was gay, in the park. Diane Feinstein called for the accused to be charged as adults. Community groups such as the Mission Real Alternatives Program, accused the police of botching the investigation and for increasing their harassment of Latino youths in the park. If anything positive came from such violent incidents, of which there were multiple, it was that it led to the Latino and gay community to work in collaboration on social issues, such as the neighborhood patrols organized by the Community United

Against Violence, a Castro community organization that monitored incidents of anti-gay violence.

However, despite the insistence of several groups that the ground was a major confrontation area for gay-Latino tensions, Mayor Feinstein said "There is no evidence of anti-gay sentiments made prior to the attack," calling such allegations "sheer baloney."

"Nowhere in the reports is there any indication these guys were out to beat up gays" said police spokesman Henry Friedlander. According to the police, the only reference to gays came from a third party "Latin" who told the arresting officers the suspect had kicked "two f---- asses for nothing."

"I got the idea there was something else bothering them," stated one of the two victims.

"This attack may have not been related, but that park has been gay for years," his friend who was visiting him in the hospital commented.

However, some differed in their assessment of the attack. One of the largest grassroot groups to be born in San Francisco in the last 50 years of the 20th century was the Community United Against Violence, composed largely of middle-class residents who were moving into neighborhoods such as the Western Addition and Mission. Formed in 1977, the group was made up of both straights and gays, and was involved in such activities as the distribution of whistles.

"I'm not willing to say it was a case of homophobia. But this scenario is typical of what we see two or three times a week at the park. We consider Dolores a hotspot of antigay harassment by Latinos," said Dick Stingel head of the CUAV

Both Latinos who lived nearby and the police who patrolled the park felt agitated by the event. Many officers felt there was nothing they could do about such instances.

"Several years ago we were given an unwritten order to stay out of there after community groups complained of police brutality. It's sad for the people who live on the edge of the park but there is not much we can do," said one task force officer.

Latino community leaders felt that the police had done enough if not overstepping their bounds already.

"The way the police reacted to the incident is typical. They arrested kids who hadn't even been involved in the assault," said Roberto Hernandez of the Mission Real Alternatives Program. "The city has nothing in terms of staffing the park for organized activities for neighborhood kids. Nothing is happening so they get involved in drugs and alcohol."

The Gay Subcommittee of the Intergroup Clearinghouse, an organization of 30 citywide, religious, ethnic, and community agencies headed by Dr. Zuretti Goosby, a black community leader and schoolboard member, in light of the incident in Dolores Park, felt it necessary to try and bring the two communities together. In a report released by the group, it advised that San Francisco's juvenile and young adult population be educated to have a greater understanding about gays, as well as for gay leaders to be educated in tenant rights and the necessity of low income housing. While the first two of its points were conciliatory, the third struck a somewhat draconian tone. "The majority of those involved with this report supported the need for a city policy on violent crimes. Depending on the type of case, there should be a standard maximum sentence and all the youths should be tried as adults."

In a study conducted by the group of 123 assaults, it was found that the average victim of anti-gay violence in San Francisco was a male walking alone at night in the Castro District within the four blocks of 18th and Castro that made up the neighborhood. Although assaults of gays did occur outside of the district, they tended to be robberies or muggings where the perpetrators were looking for passive victims. According to the report, in "the area bounded by 17th Street, Sanchez Street, 19th Street and Diamond Street, however, the data strongly support the conclusion that the assailants come into the area looking for "faggots' to beat up."

Around 1987, housing prices for the Western Mission (where Dolores Park is located) began to stagnate despite the area having undergone gentrification for the decade prior. This led to increased acrimony between homeowners in the area, many of who had bought homes during an earlier period, and did not want to see their home values fall, and other residents of the Mission who used Dolores Park. In 1992, Susan Finnegan, a resident of 19th street who ran a childcare center from her home, had her living room firebombed when she called the police on a drug deal occurring in the park.

Along with the increased speculation from middle class buyers, the Mission also took in the entry of many new residents from Central America during the first half of the 1980s. Central American immigrants made up more than 40 percent of San Francisco's growth in population during these years, doubling in number from 49,300 in 1980 to 84,600 in 1985 (in absolute numbers, San Francisco's overall population rose by 42,426 people, around 17, 000 of whom were from Central America). Notably, this number was far diminished when looking at other counties in the Bay Area. Other than San Mateo County, for which Central American immigration accounted for 30 percent of the population increase, Central American immigration did not greatly affect the population growth of any other county. The third closest was Alameda County for which it accounted for only 5.5 percent of the growth in population, less than the percentage of the increase that was due to immigration from Mexico (8.3 percent) This was due in part to the special historical relationship that San Francisco has had with Central America since the 19th Century. During the Gold Rush, the Pacific Mail Steamer and other ships would use overland passages (mostly in Panama and Nicaragua) to connect between the East Coast and San Francisco. With Coffee becoming the chief cash crop in Central America, a brisk trade developed between the West Coast and the region, with San Francisco being the chief processor. Due to this trade, the coffee companies based in San Francisco (Folger's, MJB, and Hills Brothers) created contacts in the region that led to migratory movements from Central America to San Francisco. Although at first limited to the wealthy members of the coffee plantations, mass migration increased in the early 20th century when many male workers came to work in the coffee companies, and during World War Two, many of the wartime industries recruited labor from Central America. Mexican immigrants tended to be recruited into the Bracero Program, leading them to settle more in the South and East Bay, where there was a large agriculture industry. This migratory trend, over the years would lead to San Francisco being unique in its Latino population, in that it would be in the minority of major western United States cities where, amongst the Latino population, those from or descended from people from Central America would predominate those from Mexico. Already by 1950, the Central American born population outnumbered the Mexican born population in San Francisco. In 1970, there were 18,500 Latinos in San Francisco of Mexican or Mexican American heritage, versus 27,000 who were descended from other Latin American nationalities. Latinos of Mexican heritage were only 39 percent of San Francisco's overall Latino population in 1980. Of San Francisco's Central American population, by the late 1980s, 53 percent were Salvadorian, 31 percent were Nicaraguan, and 10 percent were Guatemalan. However, although fewer in number, Latinos of Mexican origin predominated in the Mission's areas with the highest concentration of Latino's (by 1982 the area south of 19th Street), comprising almost two-thirds of all households. The influx of diverse Central American groups into the Mission in the 1980s is representative of the neighborhood's history of heterogenous population cohabitation. Unlike the Western Addition, where "white flight" preceded before African Americans became the demographic majority, the Mission's population change from being an ethnic European neighborhood to a Latino one was gradual. Arriving first in the 1930s and 40s, the Latino population of the Mission began a noticeable ascension in the 1950s, from 11 percent in 1950 to 23 percent in 1960, increasing to 45 percent of the population by 1970.

Valencia Street again underwent changes in character in the late 1980s and early 90s. From being the center of the Women's Movement in the Bay Area throughout the previous two decades, it became even more bohemian, and then chic. Perhaps the artistic roots in the western Mission (the part where Valencia Street is located) go back to what was known as the Gartland Pit, the result of a fire which cost the lives of twelve people when the Gartland Hotel on 16th and Valencia was the target of an arson in 1975. In the years after the fire, the lot which remained would become the site of a local art movement, as graffiti artist, theatre troops, poets, and film enthusiast all used it. Its development became an issue around which neighborhood organizers collaborated to prevent its conversion into an office building and fast food franchise (it eventually would become an apartment building with some low-income housing in the late 80s.)

Also contributing to the growth of artist in the North Mission was Club Komotion, which opened in 1986 on 16th Street when several local bands pooled their resources together to buy a machine shop. It would become the location of one of the Bay Area's biggest underground nightclubs where artist would come together to put on shows with little or no cover charge. The neighborhood even had its own newspaper, the North Mission News, that catered to the bohemian and progressive cultural taste of its readers. Many residents were aware however, how the neighborhood was close to or in the process of gentrifying.

"San Francisco is becoming a haven for the culturally and economically upwardly mobile. I see the trend in this neighborhood," said resident and tenant rights attorney Marc Janowitz in 1988.

"The pattern here could be similar" (to North Beach in San Francisco or SOHO in New York), agreed Maryann Dillon (director of the Mission Housing Development Corporation which organized the financing for the low income housing in the apartment building which replaced the lot where the Gartland Hotel had stood), where artist who "act as a magnet" drew in others to gentrify the area.

Artemis Bar, formerly the most prominent lesbian bar in the neighborhood, closed down in 1990. A crepe restaurant, Ticouz, opened up next to Café Picaro on 16th Street in 1992, which had concurrently transitioned from being a gritty leftist political café to an upscale Tapas Bar.

Within the same year, a Middle Eastern Falafel Shop, two cafes, a sushi restaurant, a tattoo parlor, and a four cuisine Asian restaurant, all opened at the intersection of 16th and Valencia.

By 1990, after witnessing twenty years of gentrification, community leaders in the Mission were working to preserve its Hispanic cultural heritage. Along with the demographic changes at this time that had included the growth and sustainment of the women/feminist/lesbian neighborhood along Valencia Street, interest and investments in the neighborhood from Bohemian Artist, Hong Kong Merchants, and Asian grocers, gave the neighborhood a different ambience as well. While the greater diversity was appreciated, the reality was that much of the area and population that had constituted the Latino barrio had been pushed eastwards (out of Noe Valley) and lost over the previous two decades (as mentioned the city's Latino population fell by nearly 20% from 1970-1980).

As a result, a generation of community leaders, composed of college educated organizers and merchants, came together to preserve and revitalize the Latino center of the Mission. Very central to the organizing occurring at this time was Roberto Hernandez, president of the Mission Economic and Cultural Association, who led the movement to revitalize 24th street with the ambitions of turning it into a destination much like Olvera Street in Los Angeles. Hernandez also brought the annual celebration of Brazil's Carnival to the Mission in 1979. Working with the San Francisco Convention and Visitor Center Bureau, these leaders created a brochure highlighting cultural interest and locations in the neighborhood, such as the murals in Balmy Alley and art galleries like the Galleria de la Raza. Along 24th street, flags from different Latin American countries were hung from light poles to celebrate the diversity of the Mission's Latino community, and the annual Calle 24 Festival de las Americas (24th Street Festival of the Americas) began. Efforts were also made by Hernandez and Roberto Barragan, president of the Mission Economic Development Association, to bring the Mexican Museum to the Mission. It was during the late 80s real estate boom, that many of these leaders realized an imminent danger of losing the community completely. The Mission Housing market was so hot, for example, that in 1989 Skyline Realty mailed flyers to long term property owners in the Mission, stating that they had foreign buyers lined up, with property owners only needing to name their price.

"Its not that other people aren't welcomed, but there isn't anyplace else left for us" Said Rosa Rivera, owner of El Nuevo Frulandi, a Puerto Rican restaurant on 24th street, and a neighborhood advocate.

By the late 90s, the gentrification that had begun mainly in the northern and western Mission had come to the neighborhood's central Latino area, announcing itself on the northern border along 20th Street. Locations for six of the major properties, buildings, and enterprises which were the center of controversies concerning infringement from dot-com gentrification were located within blocks of the intersection of 20th and Mission Street (the Old Bayview Bank Building, Bryant Square, Bruno's Restaurant, Foreign Cinema, the Tower Theatre Building, and the New Mission Theatre Building). Evictions in San Francisco were at an all time high, culminating in 2,386 evictions in 1998 alone. Seeing this threat, and with the battles over key areas of neighborhood infrastructure occurring, Mission District residents pushed for Proposition L, a measure that would have limited the building of office spaces in the Mission. Mayor Willie Brown and his pro-development allies spent millions to defeat it.

Although the dot-com era was responsible for social upheaval and unrest in the Mission, it was not until the years after the Bernal Dwellings and the Valencia Gardens (the Mission District's two main public housing communities) were destroyed, that the Mission's population saw major changes. The district's Latino population was stable throughout the 90s, dropping only two percentage points by the decade's end. The organization begun by Latino leaders in the early 1990s stood strongly against gentrification during the dot-com era, and prolonged the displacement of the Mission's Latino community that had begun in the 1970s by a decade. It would be the years after Hope VI was initiated and completed on the Bernal Dwellings and the Valencia Gardens, which prior to their destruction had been commonly seen as impeding the full gentrification of the area, that the Mission's Latino community would continue its decline in size and population. From being 60 percent of the Mission's population in 2000, by 2009 it accounted for 48 percent with a net loss of 27 percent of its Latino population. With the predominantly African American, minority, and low income populations of these public housing communities removed, and the structures rebuilt as less visible and with fewer units, the last apprehensions from those involved in the Mission's gentrification did as well.

Another San Francisco neighborhood which saw many influxes and transitions in the last quarter of the 20th Century was South of Market, a neighborhood south of downtown roughly defined as sitting between Market Street and King Street, from Bay Street to Twelfth Street. In 1979, the names of several streets originally named after early settlers were renamed in the neighborhood to honor heroes from Filipino history. Alice Street became Mabini Street, O'Doul Lane became Tandang Sora Street, and Maloney Street became Lapu Lapu Street (Bonifacio and Rizal Street were each respectively renames of portions of Shipley Street and Clara Street). Named after heroes in the 1890s military struggle against the Spanish (Bonificio, Mabini, and Tandang), the father of the Philippines (Jose Rizal), and the native ruler who defeated and killed Portuguese explorer Francisco Magellan (Lapu Lapu), the new names acknowledged the Filipino heritage and population that had been greatly present in the neighborhood since the first wave of Filipino immigrants (1890-1930) had come to work in the San Juaquin valley. This generation was responsible for creating the neighborhood which was originally the most populous Filipino neighborhood in San Francisco, a ten block stretch along Kearny Street known as Manilatown. The majority of this first generation were male migrant worker, many of whom became lifelong bachelors because of restrictive immigration laws, which prevented them from bringing their wives to the U.S., and the miscegenation laws, which prevented them from marrying whites. Many were eventually drawn to the South of Market neighborhood, whose already residing Mexican American and Native American population they felt welcoming and easy to assimilate into. The second wave of immigration from the Philippines came after World War Two, when the restrictive immigration laws were lifted and Filipino members of the U.S. Army were allowed to bring their families over, many settling heavily in the area around 3rd and Howard. In the late 60s, after the Immigration Act of 1965, an additional 4,000 new residents from the Philippines moved into the neighborhood, many fleeing the political oppression of the Marcos regime. Two census tracks comprising the area were around 28 percent Filipino as late as 1988. The areas around Natoma and Clemintina became heavily populated with Filipinos, with several Tagalog Newspapers and multiple Filipino groceries opening and operating in the area. The original Manilatown was eventually absorbed into San Francisco's financial district on its eastern border, the final blow to the neighborhood coming with the eviction of residents from the International Hotel in 1977.

As with the Western Addition, it was certain neighborhoods within the greater South of Market area that initially drew the interest of middle-class speculators and gentrifies to the area. Perhaps the most well-known was South Park. Reflective of the diversity which had constituted South of Market, the neighborhood in the mid-1970s was a predominantly African American neighborhood within the greater South of Market. The social changes that would eventually come to it were different than those local residents had intended when they formed the Committee to Save South Park.

"We want to prove to people that the black people down here in South Park can do something for themselves" said Cordelia Jeffers, who was very active within the committee.

The main goal which committee members had was to buy and rehabilitate the vacant buildings surrounding the park and rent them to low and middle-income families. The first building that the committee sought to purchase was the large three-story building at 96 South Park. Beginning in 1972, the committee worked with students at UC Berkley to write a proposal and raise the 90,000 dollars asked for the property. Plans were even designed by the architectural firm the Community Design Center for the block where the property lay and submitted to the Mayor's Office of Community Development. Despite these efforts, South Park would not be one of the communities that would be part of the office's program to receive federal funds for improvements.

Even with this setback, interest in improving the neighborhood from residents and allied politicians did not falter.

"We are all interested in South Park. We are talking about 200,000 or less. And it is true, the people in South Park have worked for years and received nothing." said Supervisor Bob Mendelsohn.

Optimistic about achieving the purchase of 96 South Park, committee member Ken Johnson said:

"We all know that this community is small and the people don't have money, but we have two and three generations of black families down here. Probably more than any other street in the city. And we want to stay here and build up the community ourselves."

The committee planned to use the revenues from the rents of 96 South Park to buy other properties. Reflecting on this and other potential improvements to South Park, Cordelia Jeffers said.

"Once we get started, the junkies and the winos will leave. Then we will have a decent little community again, with all kinds of people working—and welfare, black, white, and Filipino. And we did it ourselves."

Despite the drive by Jeffers, Johnson and others on the Committee to Save South Park, it wouldn't be until a group of young professionals moved to the neighborhood beginning in the early 80s that it would be viewed as having improved.

"In the 1970s, you took your life into your hands if you went there day or night" one journalist wrote in 1989.

The South Park Improvement Association was born out of this renewed interest in the neighborhood from professional homeowners. This newer association, would aim to remake South Park with a character more "European in its ambience." Restaurants such as South Park Café, which served meals under master French chef Benoit Dubuisson, were opened.

The origins of the gentile class's renewed interest in the neighborhood began after the park received $80,000 for improvements and renovations in 1972. Amidst "soul music, soul food, and soulful reminiscing" South Park was rededicated, now featuring bright red picnic tables, multi-colored benches, new landscaping and playground equipment, with acting mayor Robert Mendelsohn, Police Chief Donald Scott, and other city politicians in attendance. Mendelsohn promised the 200 or so neighborhood residence also in attendance more low rent and affordable housing in the area. Yet this promise contrasted with the reality already of many, specifically of those who resided in the Parkview Hotel nearby (who were also in attendance), all of whom were to be evicted the following month, as their rents had been raised by their landlord who was incentivized by the rennovation.

"They're gonna have to throw me out, I aint got no place to go" said J.C. Miskell, a clerk for a trucking company who had been living at the hotel for 14 years.

In the early 1980s, real estate firms such as the Breitman Company began to remake South of Market as a residential and office annex to downtown. The market cooled briefly when the oversupply of office space downtown and the recession of 1981-1983 proved disastrous for speculators who had invested in the area, but had picked up again by 1985. During this time, many art galleries, such as the Modernism, Vision, Hoover, New Langton Arts, SOMA Cafe and the Bluxome Street Gallery opened. Concurrently, there was a real estate boom for night clubs on Folsom Street, many of which were straight and replaced what had been a gay club scene between 7th and 12th Streets on Folsom known as the Folsom Street "Miracle Mile", such as the Oasis (the largest and most notable of the nightclubs which opened in South of Market during the mid-80s). Like other areas of the city which were composed of gay night clubs and theatres, such as the Polk Gulch (Polk Street between Broadway and Geary Street), many of the clubs on the Folsom Miracle Mile were closed and converted into straight clubs as social consequence to the AIDS crisis. Nightclubs were not the only businesses affected; the number of gay and lesbian businesses reached a peak in 1982, after which during the following 6 years it would fall by a quarter of the number in that year. The gay population and commercial presence in San Francisco had previously been growing since World War II, when a number of personnel from the Pacific Theatre were dishonorably discharged in the Bay Area for sexual misconduct, and many more gay veterans returned after the war.

"With the change in lifestyles—and the explosion in videos—gay theatres have lost about 50 percent of their business." Said Jim Carouba, who bought the New Century Theatre on Larkin Street near the Polk Gulch and converted it into a straight adult theatre in 1989.

The growth of San Francisco's downtown in the 1970s and 1980s was pressing on the communities of the Western Addition and Mission, which it also bordered on. The Opera Plaza Condominiums, completed in 1982 on the 600 block of Van Ness Avenue, was hailed for being an essential part of the renewal efforts on downtown and Market Street. It was the largest condominium development completed in the city until that time. Its nine percent Annual Percentage Rate, and 30-year fixed rate mortgage, made it more affordable for middle-income residents to live in San Francisco, but it was built on lands sold to the developer, the San Francisco Pacific Union Company, by the San Francisco Redevelopment Agency. Its location at the corner of Jefferson Square on the Eastern border of the Western Addition was in some ways another representation of the gentrification pressuring the Western Addition's low income communities.

The major renovation of downtown San Francisco began in the 1950s with the planning of Bay Area Rapid Transit system. It was assumed by city planners that it was in the best interest to remake Market Street since it had to be demolished anyway to create the system.

In the mid 1970s, there began an important demographic change in the Tenderloin, another San Francisco downtown neighborhood. Following Southern California communities such as Westminster (in Orange County), Vietnamese immigrants and refugees began to build communities in the Bay Area. In San Jose, more than 100 Vietnamese businesses sprang up on the edge of downtown. In San Francisco, 12,000 refugees from Vietnam and other parts of Asia settled in the Tenderloin, comprising half of the districts population, and more than 50 refugee-owned businesses were in operation, by the mid 1980s (this greatly improved a neighborhood which in 1977 had 100 vacant stores). In Westminster, the first Vietnamese owned commercial bank was created, with the Southeast Asian community in San Jose creating a similar one soon afterwards. Beginning in 1973, the wave of new refugees peaked in 1979 and 1980, when many Chinese ethnic Vietnamese joined the South Vietnamese refugees who fled the region (the resulting Asian population of the Tenderloin by 1989 would be 60-65 percent Vietnamese, 20-25 percent Cambodian and 10-15 percent Laotian). Many senior citizens were delighted to see children playing in a community previously known primarily for criminal activity and adult venture. The increase of children in the neighborhood (approximately 5,500 children in total lived within the 50 city blocks constituting the Tenderloin by the late 1980s), a result of this wave of immigration during the decade after the Vietnam War ended, led to the establishment of the first playground built in the neighborhood's 130 year history, at Eddy and Jones (Boeddeker Park).

The refugees and immigrants who made their community in the Tenderloin also dealt with the increased desirability of their neighborhood. Where at one time commercial space was so undesirable that landlords did not even charge by the square foot, commercial rents began to double what they had been only a few years earlier. Many refugee and immigrant shopkeepers (and shopkeepers of the Tenderloin generally) faced a unique problem. In their efforts to improve the buildings where their businesses were located, their desire for progress fundamentally exacerbated their eviction, as landlords were quick to replace them with businesses that could afford the increased rents. By 1984, it came to the attention of Susan Nakata, the chief business officer for the Mayor's Office of Housing and Economic Development, as being "a major problem" in the Tenderloin "exacerbated by its proximity to the downtown area."

Beginning in the early 1960s, property owners in the Potrero Hill neighborhood near to the Mission in southeastern San Francisco, began to assert themselves in ways that were often at odds with those that lived in the public housing in the neighborhood. At a meeting of the Supervisors' Finance and Planning Committee on May 9th 1962, Supervisor James Leo Haley presented a plan to sell two wartime housing projects in

Potrero Hill and Hunters Point. Although there was every indication that the board would reject his plan, regardless of the outcome he intended to bring the issue again before the full board at its meeting later in the month. Halley had won the support of more than 400 Potrero Hill residents who had submitted in a petition to the board, pushing for the city to close down the 11.5 acre Wisconsin Housing Project, one of four in the neighborhood.

"We have had enough. We don't want anymore. We see no hardship on the tenants from the gradual closing down of this project. Many can afford to live elsewhere," said a member of the Potrero Hill Boosters Association who owned a home on Kansas Street, speaking on behalf of the group.

Others, such as members of the Central Council of Civic Clubs, agreed that if the board of supervisors followed a plan to redevelop the project as middle and low income housing, they would be guilty of "perpetuating a slum in San Francisco."

Many of the other members of the Board of Supervisors were opposed Halley's plan. "Paramount must be the concern to have available low rent, decent housing for people now in these areas" said San Francisco Assemblyman Philip Burton.

Others, such as SFRA director Justin Herman, were indifferent, only noting that the project would cost about $250,000, plus the additional cost of installing a new park and school.

The San Francisco Human Rights Commission had noted, amongst other problems in Potrero Hill in 1965, were racial tensions. However, this was resented by members of the Potrero Hill Boosters Association and others, who told the commission the neighborhood had no problems the commission could really solve.

"We resent the implication that there is racial tension on the hill. We like our integrated neighborhood. We wish you gentlemen had come to us under different circumstances— like for coffee and donuts" said Mrs. Victor Fleming, then president of the association. Other problems noted were housing and jobs. The issue of housing was a divisive issue. While some feared of the public housing being sold to private developers, others felt the concentration of public housing on "the Hill", was too dense. Reverend H.W. Williams urged the commission to "think about the problem of the underprivileged boys who spend their time on the street corners because they cannot get jobs, and young girls who do worse because they lack training for fruitful employment."

The threat of evictions of low income residents also concerned many. Infront of the commission many aired their grievances and distress of cases of evictions resulting from juvenile crime in the family, dipropionate increases in rent when families salaries were raised, and excessive penalties for late payments.

There were some instances where the Potrero Hill Boosters Association worked with other neighborhood community organizations. For example, the association helped support the painting of the Potrero Hill Recreation Center, with a mural depicting athletes from the neighborhood overlooking the playground, including O.J. Simpson, in 1977. The association was concerned about eliminating empty lots in the neighborhood, such as those left over from Southern Pacific, which collected garbage. It also helped keep the scenic views of the neighborhood by opposing a large development by Southern Pacific in the Mission Bay. At other times the association was often at odds with the low income residents of the neighborhood. Of all the neighborhood groups, the Potrero Hill Boosters and Merchants Association was the only group to support the construction of 132 condominiums priced mainly for upper middle-class occupants in 1981.

"We don't need houses that are built for profit. We want houses built for low income people," said Lee Brown of the Coalition of Black Trade Unions in a fiery speech in front of the Planning Commission in 1981. His stance was supported by representatives of four other neighborhood groups also in attendance, including the League of Active Neighbors, the Potrero Hill Public Housing Tenants Association, and the Potrero Hill Community Development Corporation.

"We need more mixed income housing," said Jim Queen, the president of the Potrero Hill Community Development Corporation, who also protested the "tremendous gentrification influence of the scheme."

The issue of housing for local residents on Potrero Hill again came up in 1982. This time the association was opposed to the construction of housing, primarily because part of the development was designated to be subsidized housing. The development would be the construction of 120 privately owned townhouses costing between $50,000 and $90,000 dollars, one third were to be sold to low income residents who made no more than $24,000, one third for moderate income families making less than $30,000, and one third for middle class families with incomes up to $40,000. The homes, called Wisconsin Street, were supported by Assemblyman Art Agnos.

"In this day and age of high interest rates and gigantic sales prices for housing, the only way to reduce the price of housing for working middle class people is for the City and state to chip in. With the average price of homes at over

$150,000, developers like Wisconsin Street make a great deal of sense." said Agnos.

The rising cost of housing in San Francisco not only affected working and low-income communities in the city, but also those just north an exit across the Golden Gate Bridge in Marin County. Even white-collar professionals had to make financial decisions in light of the rise.

"I used to live in Pacific Heights but the rents kept going up and drove me out," said a college educated vice president of a property management firm. He was one of the buyers purchasing one of the 139 condominium units being built in 1979 in Marin City. "There are a hell of a lot of whites who would like to live this close to San Francisco. The blacks should feel lucky that they're in this economic vacuum, paying such low rents. Every house within 20 miles of here is going for six figures."

Marin City began as a wartime housing project during World War II. Designated to be a model for redevelopment, the County of Marin took title to all 350 flatland and ridge acres next to the highway, drawing up a masterplan for a community that would include light industry, schools, shopping areas, recreational facilities, and low and moderate income housing. In 1961, the county made an offer to New York Congressman James H. Scheuer and his company California Development Co., to develop the project. As an incentive Scheuer would receive 167 acres of scenic ridgelands for only $441,000. Ten years later, however, all that existed in Marin City were several federally funded low-income housing buildings and a gas station, isolated, and far from the comprehensive community envisioned. Scheuer's firm blamed the lack of development on tight resources and rising tensions in the predominantly black community. The federal government decided to withhold financial backing until Marin County once again took possession of the lowlands, preventing a lawsuit on behalf of the county. It's redevlopment agency, to save itself from bankruptcy and keep the project alive, presented to Scheuer another negotiation which would give him clear title to the ridgelands in exchange for the county receiving unrestricted rights to develop the lowlands Scheuer had promised to but never had. Many in Marin City were up in arms for what was perceived as a land giveaway. The county board of supervisors, over the heated protest of residents, approved it, and from then on relations were strained between the county and Marin City residents, who felt that they had no control over the development of their community.

Such preference manifested itself in the construction of the condominiums on the hillsides above Marin City in the late 1970s. Marin City residents had tried for weeks to receive better transit service for Drake Avenue, the main road running through Marin City. The unfulfillment of their request was garnished with further insult when Golden Gate Transit began providing direct service to the condominiums.

"Here we had asked for bus service and couldn't get it and the white people on the hill were getting it without even asking," said Betty Hodges, a director of the local community services district. With other residents, Hodges disrupted bus services by picketing during commute hours until their demands were met.

"All of a sudden, Marin City is a divided community. The hill is white and middle class and the flats are poor and black. The question is, how long we can survive in such an exclusive neighborhood? We're isolated here, but people know that what's happening in Marin City is happening on

Potrero Hill and Hunters Point and parts of West Oakland. It's a problem that's not unique."

A 1974 consultants report on advisable ways to market the ridgelands advocated that "every effort be made to minimize awareness of Marin City in future residents minds." Despite its publishing in the press, and its disownment by defensive redevlopment officials, the new condominium townhouses, priced between $125,000 and $190,000 and developed by Pacific Union Co., sold quickly, with more than 200 buyers filling a waiting list hoping for cancelations.

Despite the development of the hillside in the late 1970s, the flatlands where Scheuer had planned a community remained barren and weed infested. The divide between the hillside residents and those of the flatlands was softened somewhat by the construction of 40 federally subsidized units within the then new 198 Richardson Highlands apartment complex.

Clarence Swann, then the general manager of the Marin City Community Services District, felt that the survival of Marin City's low income community depended on the success of the Community Development Corporation, a non profit organization formed by him and other black leaders in the summer of 1979. The group hoped to gain enough financial backing to control ten acres of county property in front of Highway 101, then the site of the weekend Marin City Flea Market, and 32 undeveloped acres owned by the Tamalpais High School District. According to Swann, the land occupied by the flea market had attracted developers interested in building a hotel complex and regional shopping center. He and other believed that Marin City's black residents could benefit from the development of the property. by giving them an economic stake in the community that hadn't previously existed.

"The situation is analogous to discovering oil on an Indian reservation. The Indians are told they can stay on the land forever, then they discover oil and the Indians have to go. That's what's happening here now...(it's) factually true that there are no plans to eliminate public housing, but if there are $300,000 homes right above a housing project, it creates pressure...There is a definite presence of fear among the people here that they're being squeezed out of their community," said Swann. Swann and Hodges were optimistic about the development of the property where the flea market was located, however.

"We've chosen to live here because it's a community and family, and were interested in seeing that continue" said Hodges in 1979 prior to its development. "Marin City has a little over 500 families. It's a microcosm of the problems that exist in the cities. Here, these problems seem manageable. If poor people can gain ownership and control of their community, they can survive. It's an experiment."

****

Epilogue

At the end of World War Two, many African Americans who had originally come to San Francisco to work in the Naval Arms industry began settling in the Western Addition, where they built a vibrant and cosmopolitan community. African Americans had always been present in San Francisco since its early history. The 1860 census list 1,176 "free colored" (503 black and 673 mulatto) residents, approximately 2 percent of the city's population at the time. During the 1800s, most African Americans lived downtown. After the 1906 earthquake and fire, many began to move into the Western Addition. By 1920, a community of families had formed around Ellis and Scott Street. The Works Project Administration described the community in 1940:

The greater number of San Francisco's 7,000 Negroes live in the neighborhood west of Fillmore between Geary and Pine Street. Among them are representatives of every state in the Union, of Jamaica, Cuba, Panama, and South American countries. Of those from the South, the greater number are Texans who arrived after the World War; these still celebrate Juneteenth, Emancipation Day for the Texas Negroes, who did not learn of the Emancipation Proclamation until June 19, 1863. The colony's social life revolves around a handful of bars and restaurants, its one large and noisy nightclub, its eight churches of varying faiths, and the Booker T. Washington Community Center on Divisadero Street, where trained social workers guide educational and recreational activities for children and adults. Occasionally, in churches and clubs, are heard old Negro folks songs surviving the days of slavery.

This small community would be the foundation for the larger one which came into being in the 1940s and 50s. Often described as being "the Harlem of the West", clubs lined Fillmore Street (from which the Western Addition gets is colloquial namesake), such as Jimbo's Bop City, Café Society, Leola's Bird Cage, Hank's 500, the Big Glass and Barrell House, and Leola King's Blue Mirror, where entertainers Johnny Mathis, Flip Wilson and Richard Wyands began their careers. The Fillmore neighborhood, or the Western Addition, of this era, was the first neighborhood in San Francisco to taste the destruction of urban renewal during the 1950s and 1960s.

Perhaps the model for the chic neighborhood later exemplified by many gentrified San Francisco neighborhoods was Union Street. In 1952, the street which would become a heavily used commercial strip, held 45 vacant store fronts. By 1966, all of these were filled and there was a waiting list to rent. The demolition of the Western Addition during this first phase of urban renewal, and the remaking of Union Street through the 1950s and 1960s, are connected in that they would come to exemplify the neighborhood idealization targeted by city planners, developers, and investors in later years, especially those leading up to and following Silicon Valley's reawakening in the mid-1990s.

The focus of this book has been the displacement and gentrification which occurred during the last few decades of the twentieth century and into the 21st century, from the 1970s until its conclusion and into the early 2000s. As well as low income, many middle and working-class people left the city at this time, leading to the growth of communities outside of San Francisco. Throughout the 1980s, the majority of whites, Asians, and Hispanics who left San Francisco but remained in the Bay Area left for San Mateo county (33.7, 46.6, and 48.6 percent respectfully). Thirty-two point eight percent of African Americans who left San Francisco but stayed in the Bay area also went to San Mateo, helping the county grow-in size, but this was second to Alameda county, where 37.6 percent left to. Essentially, many working and ethnic communities were displaced during this time, a period that has been greatly under-researched and poorly analyzed. What has been uncovered is the fact that the displacement of San Francisco's African American, Latino, and other non- white and/or working class groups, was done with the deliberation of city planners, not just by gentrification within the private market. The housing authority created a planned, well thought-out exodus by destroying large public housing communities (North Beach-720 residents/229 units; Plaza East- 640 residents/276 units; Hayes Valley North and South 620 residents/ 294 units; Bernal Dwellings 520 residents/ 208 units; the Geneva Towers 1000 residents/576 units) and replacing them with smaller, mixed income communities, thereby aiding the gentrification that had been taking place in San Francisco since the 1970s. The renewal of San Francisco into a gentrified city for white collar workers was perhaps the goal of city planners since the earliest stages of planning for the Bay Area Transit System (BART), when planners hoped to realize their goal of turning San Francisco into a connected centralized capital for commerce of the Bay Area and Northern California. The city of San Francisco had entered into a period of economic stagnation after World War II until 1960, though it was not as apparent statistically as in other cities. Although the labor force remained constant at 331,000 jobs, the population of the city declined from 775,000 to 740,000 during the 1950s. Real estate values fell 32 percent between 1920 and 1950. What is the most apparent from this period however was the growth in the surrounding urban area in both employment and population. The outmigration of middle class white families from San Francisco to these areas can be seen in the drop in the overall number of whites in the city by 13 percent during the 1950s, while at the same time so can the growth of ethnic enclaves, as the percentage of minorities increased by 43 percent.

A number of factors led to this growth in the Bay Area suburbs. As a peninsula San Francisco was prevented from annexing peripheral growth. Both the Bay Bridge and the Golden Gate Bridge were built during the era of the New Deal. Perhaps most importantly however, was the decision of Bay Area business leaders to locate the expansion of industry in the post-war period in the suburbs. Like the relocation of industries to the South from the Northeast and Midwest, most of this was in response to the unionization of the labor force in San Francisco and Oakland. A 1946 pamphlet from the California State Reconstruction and Reemployment Commission conveys the feelings of a group of managers of small plants in the Santa Clara Valley, as it notes they:

"testify their employees are more loyal, more cooperative, more productive workers than those they have had in big cities."

A banker echoed this statements in front of the Common Wealth club in 1948 stating "Labor developments in the last decade may well be the chief contributing factor in speeding the regional dispersion of industry...Large aggregations of labor in one central city plant are more subject to outside disrupting influences, and have less happy relations with management, than in smaller suburban plants."

As a result, San Francisco's labor force remained constant while the surrounding suburbs' employment grew by 38 percent. Auto plants moved from Richmond and Oakland to Fremont; in Santa Clara, the electronics industry and defense plants expanded upon their beginnings in World War II in an area that were once rural and agricultural. Fredrick Terman, Stanford's Dean of Electrical Engineering (and the former head of the World War II MIT Radiation Laboratory) negotiated government contracts to university spawned firms such as Hewlett-Packard and Fairchild Semiconductors. In contrast, although the labor force remained constant, there was a heavy decline in labor in San Francisco's traditional manufacturing industries, the waterfront and wholesaling, and this lack of blue-collar employment manifested itself in the deterioration of central city areas. It would be the housing stock in these areas that drew the attention of city developers and politicians who created the urban renewal programs for them that would lead to their ensuing speculation and gentrification. The SFRA acquired the structures they wished to demolish. However, it moved slowly in acquiring properties, largely due to California's legislation hampering land taking by eminent domain, and the SFRA could not get its condemnation suits expedited by the city attorney's office. In the second wave of urban renewal which began in 1966, it demanded that those which were not demolished to be brought up to code, providing financing for private rehabilitation. Many absentee landlords were earnest to sell to new investors, who acquired properties for around $5,000 per unit, bringing the first wave of middle-class investors to the Western Addition and other neighborhoods.

All of these factors, however—increased speculation and gentrification, as well as planned removals of entire communities to expedite it—suggest the indication of a greater collusion to diminish and limit the growth of certain communities. Was the Hope VI program the final phase of a process of gentrification? Hopefully, this book has provided a historical overview of the manner by which ethnic and culturally distinct neighborhoods were gentrified over a process of 30 years, by both government and private means. It was a process which involved coercion, misrepresentation, and sometimes violence. The public housing communities eventually destroyed and minimized by Hope VI and other redevelopment projects, organized to assert themselves and improve their environments, despite the opposition they faced to even exist.

The scene of the large-scale raid conducted on the 500 block of Haight Street (between Steiner and Fillmore), in the Lower Haight Ashbury, on Thursday November 3, 1977. More than 100 people, including children and infants, were removed from their homes and herded into the foyer of an abandoned movie theatre at 560 Haight Street. **88**

Photograph by Peter Breinig

Two men, one a protestor (right) of the rebuild of Yerba Buena
Plaza West and one a supporter (left), argue in front of its
buildings at the date commencing its demolition, Thursday
August 17th 1989. Whilst housing authority president, Lewis
Lillian, and executive director David Gilmore, gave speeches
filled with combative metaphors to convey the struggle with
which it took to get the public housing community rebuilt
after its demolition, a delegation of protestors made up of
various property owners and organized by PADS (Planning
Association for Divisadero Street) had met and clashed with its
supporters. **82**

Photograph by Bryant Ward

A marching band makes its way down Page Street in the Haight-Ashbury, circa 1972. The neighborhood's population was over a third African American in 1970.

From Assignment Four: *What's Happening in the Haight*, 1972. 22:32. KRON TV. Young Broadcasting of San Francisco, Inc. Bay Area Television Archive.

Yerba Buena Annex circa 1964.

San Francisco History Center, San Francisco Public Library

Photograph by Alan J. Canterbury

Yerba Buena Plaza Annex, colloquially known as "the Pink Palace", 1982.

San Francisco History Center, San Francisco Public Library

Photograph by Larry Moon

Yerba Buena Plaza East at Laguna and Turk Street, 1964.

San Francisco History Center, San Francisco Public Library

Photograph by Alan J. Canterbury

The playground of Plaza East at Laguna and Eddy Street, 1964.

San Francisco History Center, San Francisco Public Library

Photograph by Alan J. Canterbury

The Geneva Towers, each 23 stories, provided 576 units to at least 1,000 low income people (mid 1990's estimate).

San Francisco History Center, San Francisco Public Library

Hayes Valley South, 1964

San Francisco History Center, San Francisco Public Library

Photograph by Alan J. Canterbury

Photographs of Hayes Valley, prior to and just after the removal of the section of Highway 101 (1989-1995) that went through the neighborhood.

Page Street and Octavia Street

Hayes Street and Gough Street.

Hickory Street and Octavia Street

Hayes Street and Franklin Street

Buchanan Street and Hayes Street, during the removal of the 101 on-ramp.

Hayes Street and Laguna Street, after the demolition of the 101 section (1995)

Photographs by Robert Durden

Plaza East just prior to its demolition, from the intersection of Turk and Laguna Street, circa 1995.

Plaza East when rebuilt in 2003. All of the public housing communities that would be redeveloped under Hope VI in the late 1990s would be done so with more or less identical structures as these, that were smaller and less visible than those which they replaced.

One of the towers of Yerba Buena Plaza West, 1983. A relic of
the original building still exist, the metal horse jungle gym
(seen in the bottom right corner of this photograph), is now
placed outside of a community garden in the new
developments (following page).

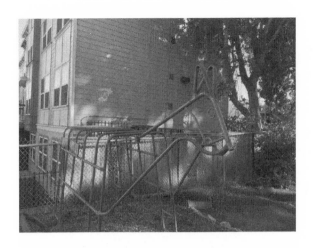

(Top three photographs) Yerba Buena Plaza West (now Robert Pitts Plaza, 2020)

Photographs by author

A plaque dedicated to Dr. Oscar J. Jackson in the Central Haight. After World War Two, many African American professionals lived and established businesses within the Haight Ashbury.

Photograph by author

Map 1

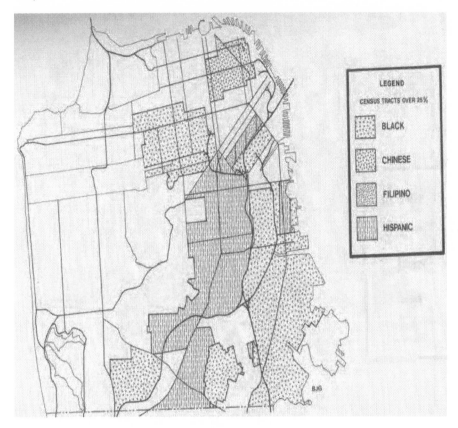

A map showing San Francisco's Black, Chinese, Filipino, and Hispanic neighborhoods, 1970.

Original Source U.S. Census.

Map 2

A map showing the same San Francisco demographics as Map
1, only in 1980. As can be seen, the western border of the
Western Addition and the Mission District had each been
pushed much further east within ten years.

Original Source U.S. Census

The Winterland Ballroom, located at the corner of Post Street and Steiner Street, in the late 1970s and during its demolition in 1979.

Photographs by Craig Lee

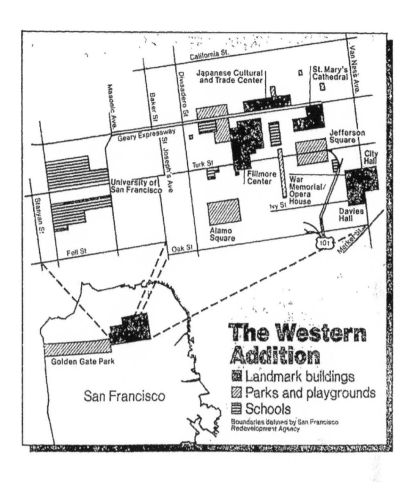

The Western Addition

■ Landmark buildings
▨ Parks and playgrounds
☰ Schools

Boundaries defined by San Francisco Redevelopment Agency

123

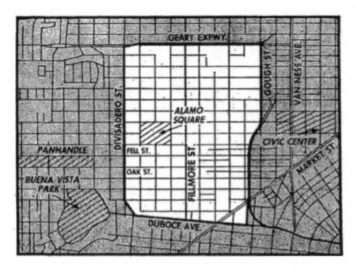

A closer view of the area that historically defined the Western Addition (top), and the area as defined by 1982. *San Francisco Chronicle*, 26 Jan. 1986, Five Star, p. 12.

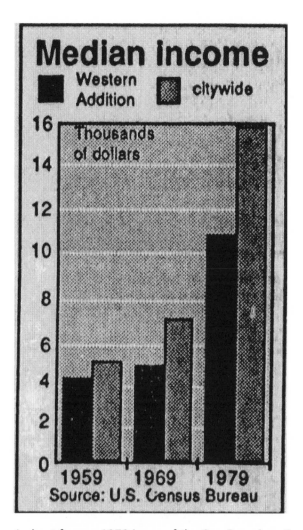

A chart from a 1979 issue of the San Francisco Examiner showing the increase in the median income of both the Western Addition and San Francisco over a 20 year period.

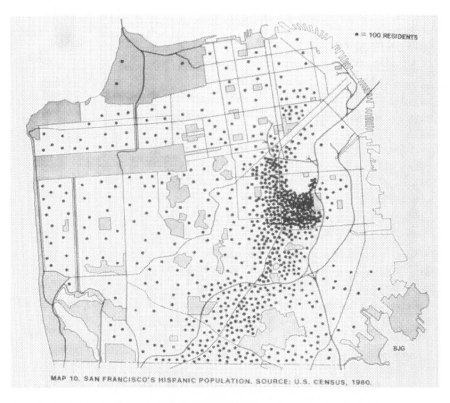

MAP 10. SAN FRANCISCO'S HISPANIC POPULATION. SOURCE: U.S. CENSUS, 1980.

San Francisco's Latino population, 1980.

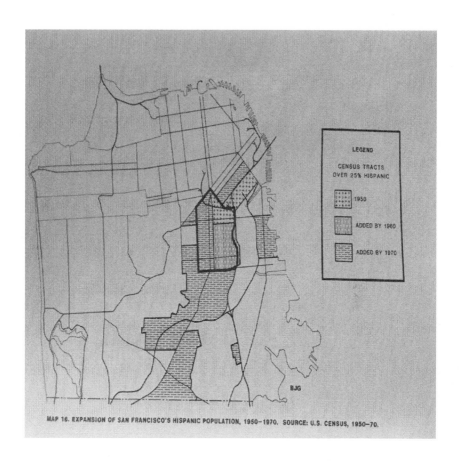

MAP 16. EXPANSION OF SAN FRANCISCO'S HISPANIC POPULATION, 1950–1970. SOURCE: U.S. CENSUS, 1950–70.

The expansion of San Francisco's Latino population 1950-1970. After World War Two, San Francisco's Latino population expanded from Howard Street in South of Market to 16th Street by 1950. From 1950 until 1960, it moved south stopping approximately by the end of the decade at Cesar Chavez Street. During the 1960s, it spread west into Noe Valley and south into Bernal Heights and the Outer Mission. Most of the Latino population displaced during the 1970s (17 percent of the total population) was from Noe Valley and other areas expanded into during the 1960s.

127

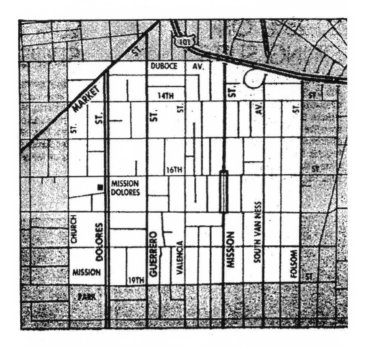

A map detailing the streets encomposing what was known as "the North Mission", 1982.

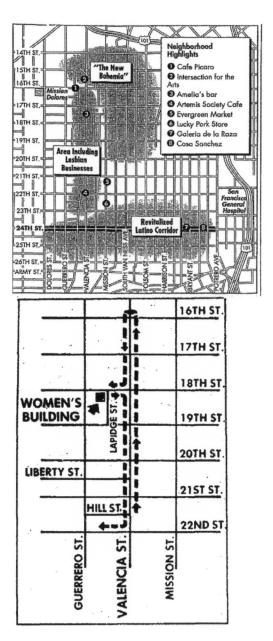

(Previous page) A map showing the three different communities that existed within the Mission by 1990. A

second which shows the location of the women's district with the location of the Women's Building featured.

TABLE 10

Housing Characteristics in the Mission District, 1980

	Mission District Core	North Mission District	West Mission District	Total Mission District	Total S.F. Citywide
Percent of Units Owner-Occupied	17.4%	4.5%	11.1%	13.3%	31.8%
Percent of Owners Hispanic	39.3%	31.8%	15.1%	31.7%	8.5%
Median Value of Owner-Occupied Homes	$91,500	$87,500	$119,900	$94,900	$103,900
Percent of Units Renter-Occupied	82.6%	95.4%	88.9%	86.7%	68.2%
Percent of Renter Households Hispanic	48.0%	34.3%	23.0%	36.7%	9.5%
Median Monthly Contract Rent	$222	$185	$250	$223	$266

Source: U.S. Census, various years. The Mission District Core includes census tracts 208, 209, 228, and 229; the North Mission, 177 and 201; and the West Mission, 202, 207, and 210.

A table detailing the socio-economic differences of the three areas of the Mission District, from the 1980 census.

Source: Census 2000, Social Explorer

A map showing the demographics of the Mission District in the year 2000.

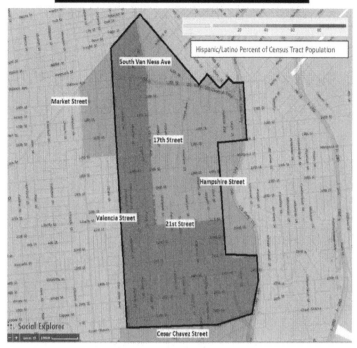

Exhibit 4: Mission District Hispanic/Latino Share of Population, 2009-2013

Source: American Community Survey 2013 (5-Year Estimate), Social Explorer

A map showing the same neighborhood demographic boundaries but for approximately the years 2009-2013.

A political cartoon from the Mission District's local newspaper, *El Tecolote*, titled "Housing, another neighborhood breaker", satires the gentrification the began to impact the neighborhood and its residents in the 1970s. The father remarks in Spanish "Good trip, we're moving in with your brother in Oakland."

(El Tecolote, February 1978)

Group	1940		1950		1960		1970		1980	
White	602,701	95.0%	693,888	89.5%	604,403	81.6%	409,285	57.2%	402,131	59.2%
Black	4,846	0.8	43,502	5.6	74,383	10.0	96,078	13.4	86,190	12.7
Chinese	17,782	2.8	24,813	3.2	36,445	4.9	58,696	8.2	82,244	12.1
Japanese	5,280	0.8	5,579	0.7	9,464	1.3	11,705	1.6	12,461	1.8
Filipino	3,483	0.5	See "Others"		12,327	1.7	24,694	3.5	38,690	5.6
Hispanic	No Data		No Data		51,602	7.0	101,901	14.2	84,194	12.4
American Indian	224	0.0	331	0.0	1,068	0.1	2,900	0.4	3,566	0.5
Others	220	0.0	7,244	0.9	2,226	0.3	10,415	1.5	53,622	7.9
Total	634,536	99.9	775,357	99.9	740,316	99.9	715,674	100.0	678,974	99.8

(Above) A table which gives the number and percentage for different ethnic/racial groups in San Francisco from 1940 to 1980. From 1970 to 1980, approximately 10,000 African Americans would leave San Francisco, mostly from the Haight Ashbury, Lower Haight, Pacific Heights, and other sections of the Western Addition. The other group for whom both the nominal and percentage numbers would decrease during the decade were Hispanics/Latinos. In terms of actual numbers lost, the group which was the most affected were Latinos, who were pushed out of Noe Valley and the adjacent areas of the Mission. However, the neighborhood's historic ties to Central America, which influenced an immigration spike to it from this region in the early 1980s as many of these nations grappled with civil wars and internecine conflicts, prevented this depletion from being as permanent until the early 2000s (a net loss then occurred of 27 percent as Latinos went from being 60 percent to 48 percent of the Mission District's population between 2000 and 2009).

(Source US Census)

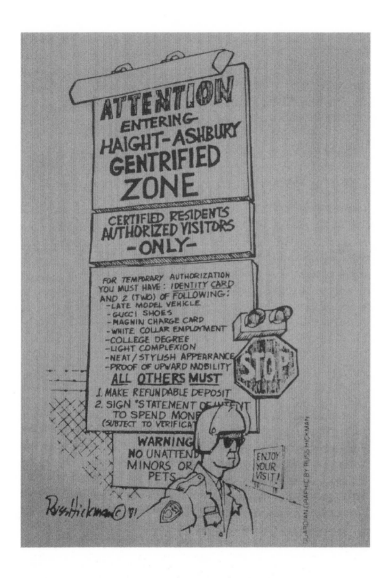

A depiction (by artist Russ Hickman) of the gentrification which the Haight Ashbury underwent during the 1970s and continuing into the 1980s.

San Francisco Bay Guardian, January 6, 1982.

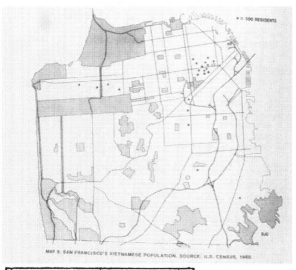

MAP 9. SAN FRANCISCO'S VIETNAMESE POPULATION. SOURCE: U.S. CENSUS, 1980.

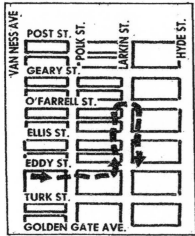

A map showing the location of San Francisco's Vietnamese population, seen here to be concentrated in the Tenderloin and Lower Nob Hill, 1980. A second shows the main commercial area of the Tenderloin's Vietnamese and South East Asian population along Larkin Street.

After the Stock Market Crash of 1929, many former single-family Victorians were converted to multiunit buildings.

The image of the Victorian Home was further blemished through pop culture references, which often depicted them as haunted. Perhaps the most influential image to reinforce this sentiment was the Adams Family. Above is the first depiction of the family's home from the November 10th, 1945 issue of The New Yorker magazine.

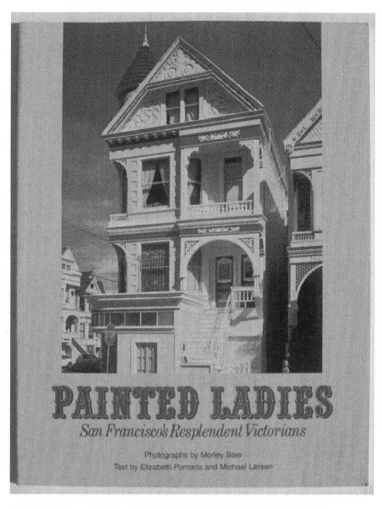

Publications such as Elizabeth Pomada's *Painted Ladies*, helped to re-popularize the Victorian.

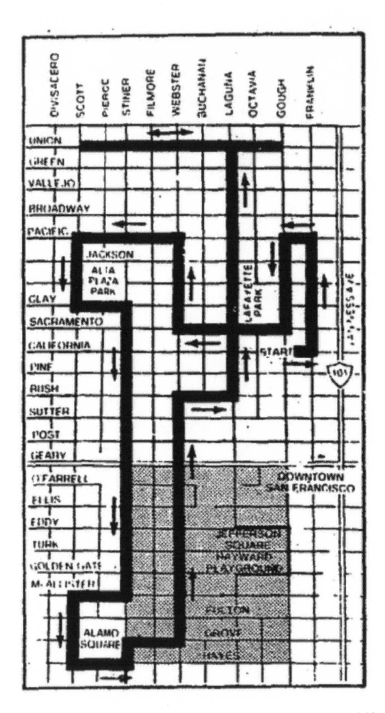

142

A map published by the San Francisco Visitors and Convention Bureau until 1981, locating the Victorians in the Western Addition. Representatives of the Police and Mayors office felt that maps such as these led to tourist muggings, such as those that strongly influenced the closer of Yerba Buena Annex.

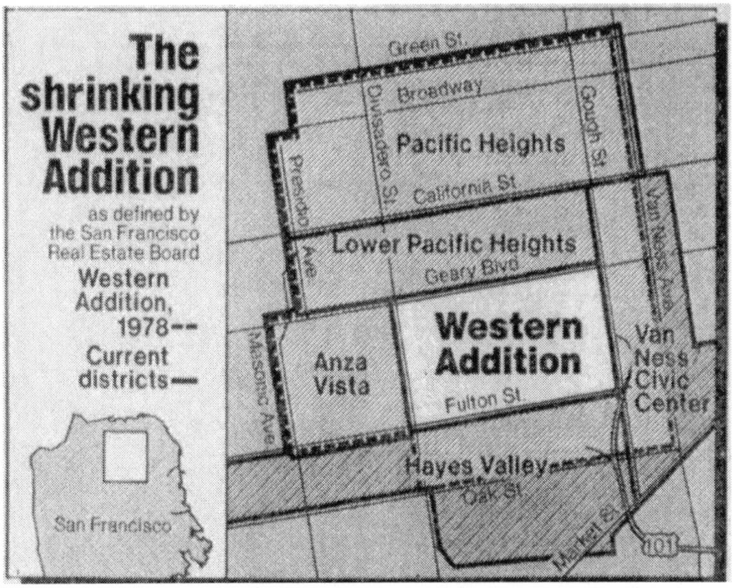
The shrinking Western Addition
as defined by the San Francisco Real Estate Board
Western Addition, 1978
Current districts
San Francisco
Green St.
Broadway
Pacific Heights
Gough St
Divisadero St
Presidio Ave
California St
Lower Pacific Heights
Van Ness Ave
Geary Blvd
Western Addition
Anza Vista
Masonic Ave
Van Ness Civic Center
Fulton St
Hayes Valley
Oak St
Market St
101

A 1986 map comparing the Western Addition's boundaries and the emergence of new neighborhoods such as Lower Pacific Heights with the neighborhoods boundaries in 1978, as defined by the San Francisco Real Estate Board.

Yerba Buena Annex, from the north looking south, 1977. Like Ping Yuen in Chinatown, the building featured exposed balconies.

Housing Furor

PINK PALACE RESIDENT NICOLE PARÉ
She feared being sent to live in a remote area of the city

THE REV. LEROY GAINS
He urged improvements

BESSIE COMBS OBJECTED TO THE PROPOSAL
She said the housing project needs fixing up

Pink Palace Residents Protest Conversion Plan

Photographs from the August 13th, 1981 San Francisco
Housing Authority meeting to discuss the conversion of Yerba
Buena Annex into senior-only housing. Despite all residents at
the meeting voicing opposition to the conversion, the SFHA
Commissioners would vote unanimously for it.

Photographs by Peter Breinig

146

Yerba Buena Plaza West after being closed and having had its previous residents removed, 1983. From 1983-1989 the three buildings that consisted of the development remained vacant before being demolished.

Photograph by David Glass

A depiction of the plan for the Fillmore Center on blocks left vacant from redevelopment. At the location where the center would be built, six blocks constituting fifteen acres along Fillmore Street had remained empty, and a contention of local interest, for nearly twenty years. Two of Yerba Buena Plaza West's three buildings can be seen in the foreground while those of Plaza East can be seen in the background.

An aerial photograph of Fillmore Street between Turk and Geary, 1975, showing the vacant lots that the Fillmore Center would eventually occupy.

Photograph by Terry Schmitt

Western Addition residents work the community gardens that existed in the lots where the Fillmore Center was eventually built, circa 1986.

Photograph by Craig Lee.

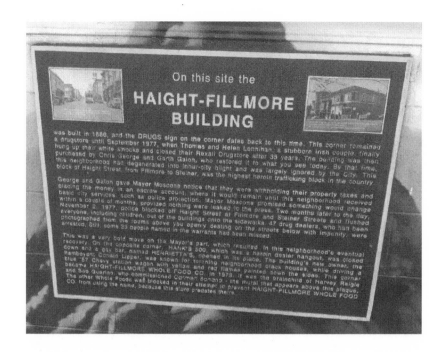

A plaque on the Fillmore Street side the Haight-Fillmore building, 2017, which gives a pro gentrification account of the building's and intersection's history.

Photograph by Author

Marvin Dumas (left photo) and Eugene Burger (right).

A poster for the October 4th , 1964 concert of Little Richard at the Fillmore Auditorium. (Above) A photograph of a young Jimi Hendrix playing with Richard at the performance.

Jimbo's Bop City, started by Charles Sullivan, was located at Post Street and Fillmore Street. Although it began as a Waffle House, it became a nightclub that would house the acts of the most luminary contemporary musicians of its time (shown on the following pages).

Louis Armstrong (first photograph) and Charlie Parker (bottom photograph) at Jimbo's Bop City.

Photographs by Stephen Jackson Jr.

Miles Davis (standing near the piano) and Dizzy Gillespie
(front-left) at Bop City. Photograph by Stephen Jackson Jr.

Sammy Davis Jr. at Bop City. Photograph by Stephen Jackson
Jr.

Louis Armstrong (center), at the Blue Mirror in the early 50s. Leola King, the owner of the Blue Mirror, is standing to the right of Armstrong.

Ella Fitzgerald at the Booker T. Washington Hotel.

Duke Ellington at the Manor Plaza Hotel, the other major hotel in the Fillmore. Both the Manor Plaza Hotel and the Booker T. Washington Hotel served African Americans visiting San Francisco, including celebrities, who were barred from using hotels downtown and in other parts of the city.

The artwork inside of the Texas Playhouse showed the Texas roots of many of the émigré house musicians and others who played at the club.

All previous photographs of the Western Addition jazz club scene, from pages 145-151 (including the poster and photograph of Little Richard and Jimi Hendrix), are from the book *Harlem of the West* (2006, Heydey Press), by Elizabeth Pepin Silva and Lewis Watts.

A block of the Western Addition razed for redevelopment. This section is near where Buena Vista Plaza East was constructed. Behind the rubble can be seen St. Mark's Lutheran Church, whose congregation and building were established and constructed in 1849.

Residents of the of the Saint Francis Square co-op pose for a photograph during a 30th anniversary celebration in 1993.

Photograph by Paul Chinn

An advertisement for the Geneva Towers, 1975.

London Breed, elected mayor of San Francisco in 2018, is perhaps the most famous of all previous residents raised in the Buena Vista Plaza East public housing community. This photograph is of a mural of her and one of the former buildings in a park in the Western Addition called the Buchanan Street Mall.

Mural by Clifton Hyson

Photograph by author

Geneva Tower residents dance in front of the buildings at a farewell party prior to its demolition, 1995.

Photograph by Craig Lee

Bibliography

1.5 Million Fire Called Arson (1983, Apr 9). San Francisco Chronicle, p. 12.

San Francisco Chronicle, 9 Apr. 1983, Four Star, p. 12.

A Spotty New Wave of Young People Moving Back to Cities. San Francisco Chronicle, 22 Jul. 1984, Sports final Five Star, p. 61.

(1984, Jul 22). San Francisco Chronicle, p. 61.

An Attempt to Humanize SF Project. (1988, Jun 25). San Francisco Chronicle, p. 2.

San Francisco Chronicle, 25 Jun. 1988, Six Star, p. 2.

Adams, Gerald. Dormant Fillmore shopping area a victim of urban undevelopment. August 16, 1978 (page 65 of 96). (1978, Aug 16). *The San Francisco Examiner*

Adams, Gerald. Reactivated Plaza West Stirs Concerns. April 8, 1988 (page 15 of 96). (1988, Apr 08). *The San Francisco Examiner*

Anders, Corey M. A hard look/Pink Palace Options that other cities have tried August 12, 1981 (page 1 of 108). (1981, Aug 12). *The San Francisco Examiner*

Anders, Corrie M. A Second Look/Farwells to Palace tinged with nostalgia, relief. November 16, 1981 (page 1 of 64). (1981, Nov 16). *The San Francisco Examiner*

Anders, Corrie M. Mayor's Palace proposal; Housing for elderly in Western Addition. July 13, 1981 (page 1 of 56). (1981, Jul 13). *The San Francisco Examiner*

Anders, Corrie M. Prisoners of the Pink Palace. June 17, 1981 (page 1 of 124). (1981, Jun 17). *The San Francisco Examiner*

Angry SF Tenants Invade Mill Valley (1974, Mar 17). San Francisco Chronicle, p. 2.

San Francisco Chronicle, 17 Mar. 1974, Five Star FINAL Late Sports, p. 2.

Assignment Four: *What's Happening in the Haight*, 1972. 22:32. KRON TV. Young Broadcasting of San Francisco, Inc. Bay Area Television Archive.

Bartlett, Robert. *Cops Sweep S.F. Block, 54 Arrested.* (1977, Nov 3). *San Francisco Chronicle*, p. 1.

San Francisco Chronicle, 3 Nov. 1977, Four Star, p. 1.

Bess, Donovan. A Paradise For the City's Elderly. 1961, Sep 24). San Francisco Chronicle, p. 30.

San Francisco Chronicle, 24 Sep. 1961, FINAL One Star, p. 30.

Beverly, Stephen. New Look in the Haight. (1975, Jun 26). San Francisco Chronicle, p. 20.

San Francisco Chronicle, 26 Jun. 1975, Four Star FINAL, p. 20.

Bizjak, Tony. San Francisco's New Bohemia. San Francisco Chronicle, 28 Dec. 1988, Six Star, p. 27.

(1988, Dec 28). San Francisco Chronicle, p. 27.

Blum, Walter. Filipinos: A Question of Identity. San Francisco Chronicle, 21 Mar. 1982, Four Star, p. 294.

Bowman, Catherine. Shioya, Tara. Public Housing Upheaval Brewing in S.F. 1994, Aug 1). San Francisco Chronicle, p. 4.

Bowman, Catherine. Painful Moves for SF Tenants (1996, Mar 25). San Francisco Chronicle, p. 13.

San Francisco Chronicle, 25 Mar. 1996, SPORTS FINAL, p. 13.

(1988, Dec 28). San Francisco Chronicle, p. 28.

Bowman, Catherine. S.F. Housing Agency Could Lose 50 Million. San Francisco Chronicle, 10 Feb. 1995, SPORTS FINAL, p. 26.

(1995, Feb 10). San Francisco Chronicle, p. 26.

Brazil, Erik. 1 Year Later: Power to the Projects. (1991, Aug 4). San Francisco Chronicle, p. 25.

San Francisco Chronicle, 4 Aug. 1991, SPORTS FINAL, p. 25.

Brian J. Godfrey. *Neighborhoods in Transition: The Making of San Francisco's Ethnic and Non Conformist Communities.* University of California Press. 1988

Budget and Legislative Analyst's Office. Policy Analysis Report. Displacement in the Mission. October 27, 2015. https://sfbos.org/sites/default/files/FileCenter/Documents/54 068-BLA.MissionDisplacement.102715.Final.pdf

Butler, Katie. Arson Nightmare in S.F. (1976, Dec 29). San Francisco Chronicle, p. 2.

San Francisco Chronicle, 29 Dec. 1976, Four Star, p. 2.

Butler, Katy. Gays Who Invested in the Black Areas.

(1979, Sep 1). San Francisco Chronicle, p. 4.

San Francisco Chronicle, 1 Sep. 1979, Four Star, p. 4.

Butler, Katy. SF Latinos to Help Gays Patrol Streets. (1981, Jan 14). San Francisco Chronicle, p. 2.

(1982, Oct 3). San Francisco Chronicle, p. 345.

Canter, Donald. Fillmore Center: A Test for Discrimination (1971, Aug 1). San Francisco Chronicle, p. 83.

San Francisco Chronicle, 1 Aug. 1971, Five Star FINAL Late Sports, p. 83.

Champion, Dale. The Battle of Alamo. San Francisco Chronicle, 6 Mar. 1972, Four Star FINAL, p. 24.

(1972, Mar 6). San Francisco Chronicle, p. 24.

Chung, L.A. New Life for the Tenderloin. (1984, Jul 5). San Francisco Chronicle, p. 1.

Chung, L.A. S.F. Agency Sued Over Hayes Valley Project Crime. (1990, Apr 24). San Francisco Chronicle, p. 37.

San Francisco Chronicle, 24 Apr. 1990, Six Star, p. 37.

City Shopping (1984, Jul 15). San Francisco Chronicle, p. 242.

San Francisco Chronicle, 15 Jul. 1984, Sports Final Five Star, p. 242.

Cops Back on Haight Hunting Pushers. 1977, Nov 4). *San Francisco Chronicle*, p. 16.

San Francisco Chronicle, 4 Nov. 1977, Four Star, p. 16.

Construction Begins on Opera Plaza. (1980, Sep 21). San Francisco Chronicle, p. 53.

San Francisco Chronicle, 21 Sep. 1980, Sports final Four Star, p. 53.)

Craib, Ralph. Aid for Housing At Brink. San Francisco Chronicle, 21 Dec. 1972, Four Star FINAL, p. 5.

(1972, Dec 21). San Francisco Chronicle, p. 5.

Curiel, Johnathan. Slice of Heaven: former high-rise form hell residents open new door. (2000, Apr 28). *San Francisco Chronicle*, p. 24.

San Francisco Chronicle, 28 Apr. 2000, SPORTS FINAL, p. 24.

David P. Varady, Wolfgang F. E. Preiser, Francis P. Russell. *New Directions in Urban Public Housing.* Center for Urban Policy Research. Routledge. Taylor and Francis Group. New York and London. 2017. First published by Transaction Publishers 1998.

Doss, Margot Patterson. The Women's District. San Francisco Chronicle, 13 Mar. 1983, Four Star, p. 128.

(1983, Mar 13). San Francisco Chronicle, p. 128.

Drewes, Caroline. Hayes Valley: A Report on the Neighborhood. (1982, Feb 21). San Francisco Chronicle, p. 103.

San Francisco Chronicle, 21 Feb. 1982, Sports final Four Star, p. 103.

Espinosa, Suzanne. Herscher, Elaine. Drugs Make Dolores Park Nightmare for Neighbors. (1992, Sep 4). San Francisco Chronicle, p. 23.

False HOPE: A Critical Assessment of the Hope VI Public Housing Redevelopment Program. June 2002. National Housing Law Project. Oakland California

Fillmore Center Scaled Down (1974, Jan 10). San Francisco Chronicle, p. 3.

San Francisco Chronicle, 10 Jan. 1974, Four Star FINAL, p. 3.

From Public Housing To Regulated Public Environments: The Redevelopment of San Francisco's Public Housing. Jane Rongerude. Department of City and Regional Planning. University of California Berkley April 1, 2007

Gay Movement remembered in S.F. exhibits. (2002, March 25). *San Francisco Chronicle*, p. 2.

Garcia, Dawn. "Low-Income Town-houses OKd". (1988, Apr 15). San Francisco Chronicle, p. 3.

San Francisco Chronicle, 15 Apr. 1988, Six Star, p. 3.

Garofoli, Joe. Mission Divided. San Francisco Chronicle, 8 Jul. 2002, SPORTS FINAL, p. 1.

(2002, Jul 8). San Francisco Chronicle, p. 1.

Garcia, Dawn. Chung, L.A.. Many Hispanics Fear Mission District is Losing Latin Flavor. San Francisco Chronicle, 3 Dec. 1990, SPORTS FINAL, p. 4.

Garcia, Dawn. Chung, L.A.. Many Hispanics Fear Mission District is Losing Latin Flavor. (1990, Dec 3). San Francisco Chronicle, p. 5.

San Francisco Chronicle, 3 Dec. 1990, SPORTS FINAL, p. 5.

Grappling with the Immigrant Experience. 1988, May 8). San Francisco Chronicle, p. 274.

Gwendolyn, Evans. Black Leaders Call Housing the Real Issue. (1979, Sep 1). San Francisco Chronicle, p. 4.

San Francisco Chronicle, 1 Sep. 1979, Four Star, p. 4.

Garcia, Ken. Mission Bears Brunt of New Wave. San Francisco Chronicle, 23 Nov. 2000, SPORTS FINAL, p. 48. (2000, Nov 23). San Francisco Chronicle, p. 48.

Garcia, Dawn. Fillmore Rebirth-Project Adds Finishing Touch. (1987, Aug 18). San Francisco Chronicle, p. 4.

San Francisco Chronicle, 18 Aug. 1987, Six Star, p. 4.

The Gay Migration into Black Neighborhoods (1979, Sep 1). San Francisco Chronicle, p. 5.

San Francisco Chronicle, 1 Sep. 1979, Four Star, p. 5.

Giteck, Lenny. Speculators and the gay housing boom. November 20, 1978 (page 25 of 72). (1978, Nov 20). *The San Francisco Examiner (1902-2007)*

Haight Renewal Panel. (1970, October 16). *San Francisco Chronicle*, p. 42.

33.) Haight: Hoping to Emerge from the Shadow. (1994, Oct 24). San Francisco Chronicle, p. 39.

San Francisco Chronicle, 24 Oct. 1994, SPORTS FINAL, p. 39.

Hall, Carl T. Growing Latin Immigration. San Francisco Chronicle, 27 Feb. 1988, Six Star, p. 2.

(1988, Feb 27). San Francisco Chronicle, p. 2.

Hamilton, Mildred. From Hippie to Yuppie. (1985, February 10). *San Francisco Chronicle*, p. 115.

Hamilton, Mildred. The Women's Building; an Update. (1980, Mar 2). San Francisco Chronicle, p. 103.

San Francisco Chronicle, 2 Mar. 1980, Four Star Final Sports, p. 103.

Hamlin, Jesse. New Look for Polk Gultch Porn Row. San Francisco Chronicle, 20 May 1989, Six Star, p. 42.

Howze, Karen. Pollard, Veronica. Saving a Street of Dreams. (1975, Dec 8). San Francisco Chronicle, p. 4.

How Housing Cost Drive People From S.F. (1985, September 18). *San Francisco Chronicle*, p. 12.

Hsu, Evelyn. North Mission: Finding a Place in the Sun. (1982, Mar 19). San Francisco Chronicle, p. 45.

San Francisco Chronicle, 19 Mar. 1982, Four Star, p. 45.

Hsu, Evelyn. Pink Palace For Seniors Ok'd. (1981, Aug 28). San Francisco Chronicle, p. 1.

Hsu, Evelyn. Pink Palace Residents Protest Conversion Plan (1981, Aug 14). San Francisco Chronicle, p. 4.

Howard, Amy L. *More Than Shelter: Activism and Community in San Francisco Public Housing.* 2014. University of Minnesota Press p.231.

Inman, Bradley. Eclectic Fillmore Neighborhood Changing Everyday (1987, Aug 16). San Francisco Chronicle, p. 64.

San Francisco Chronicle, 16 Aug. 1987, FINAL, p. 64.

Inman, Bradley. Mid-Divisadero, An Area in Transition. (1987, Jan 25). San Francisco Chronicle, p. 64.

San Francisco Chronicle, 25 Jan. 1987, Final, p. 64.

Interim Assessment of the Hope VI Program: Case Study of Bernal Dwellings and Plaza East in San Francisco, California. Final Report, volume 1, March 2003, www.abtassociates.com/reports/20039785103 68878.pdf.

Jacobs, John. Winterland's autumn years: a push to tear it down. September 26, 1978 (page 61 of 80). (1978, Sep 26). *The San Francisco Examiner.*

Kilduff, Marshal. Action on Arts Center Garage. *San Francisco Chronicle*, 30 Nov. 1977, Four Star, p. 15.

(1977, Nov 30). *San Francisco Chronicle*, p. 15.

Kamin, Ira. Changing Times on Fillmore. (1979, Aug 12). *San Francisco Chronicle*, p. 269.

San Francisco Chronicle, 12 Aug. 1979, Final Four Star Sports, p. 269.

Kilduff, Marshall. Giant Project Could Change the Fillmore. (1985, Aug 5). San Francisco Chronicle, p. 4.

San Francisco Chronicle, 5 Aug. 1985, Six Star, p. 4.

Kilduff, Marshall. Worse Than Jail (1983, Apr 9). San Francisco Chronicle, p. 4.

Lang, Parker. Lower Fillmore: Sharp Contrast From an Area Risen From the Ashes. (1982, Mar 12). San Francisco Chronicle, p. 42.

San Francisco Chronicle, 12 Mar. 1982, Four Star, p. 42.

Lassiter, Mike. New Grassroots militants: the middle class February 8, 1982 (page 13 of 60). (1982, Feb 08). *The San Francisco Examiner*

Liebert, Larry. Eyesore in the Western Addition. (1975, Jun 24). San Francisco Chronicle, p. 4.

San Francisco Chronicle, 24 Jun. 1975, Four Star FINAL, p. 4.

Long Gone—Shops , Jazz Clubs. (1975, Jun 24). San Francisco Chronicle, p. 4.

San Francisco Chronicle, 24 Jun. 1975, Four Star FINAL, p. 4.

McCabe, Michael. The Ten. (1989, Dec 31). San Francisco Chronicle, p. 110.

San Francisco Chronicle, 31 Dec. 1989, SPORTS FINAL, p. 110.

McCabe, Michael. Kids Tenderize the Tenderloin. (1987, Apr 21). San Francisco Chronicle, p. 1.

San Francisco Chronicle, 21 Apr. 1987, Six Star, p. 1.

New Meeting on Fillmore Center Issue. (1974, Nov 19). San Francisco Chronicle, p. 14.

Neighborhood at a Glance: mid Divisadero. (1987, Jan 25). San Francisco Chronicle, p. 69.

San Francisco Chronicle, 25 Jan. 1987, Final, p. 69.

San Francisco Chronicle, 28 Aug. 1981, Four Star, p. 1.

Nolte, Carl. Exotic New Street Names. San Francisco Chronicle, 28 Dec. 1979, Four Star, p. 4.

Opera Plaza has the Corner on Culture. (1982, May 2). San Francisco Chronicle, p. 347.

Peace Pact at the Geneva Towers (1974, May 29). San Francisco Chronicle, p. 3.

Power, Keith. The New Geneva Towers. (1975, Apr 16). San Francisco Chronicle, p. 13.

San Francisco Chronicle, 9 Apr. 1983, Four Star, p. 4.

Rapaport, Richard. San Francisco's SOHO? San Francisco Chronicle, 17 Mar. 1985, Sports final, p. 299.

(1985, Mar 17). San Francisco Chronicle, p. 299.

(1989, May 20). San Francisco Chronicle, p. 42.

Rally to Save Filipino Business Hub. San Francisco Chronicle, 14 Dec. 2000, SPORTS FINAL, p. 75.

Residents Near Crime Ridden S.F. Housing Projects Win Claim. (1990, May 1). San Francisco Chronicle, p. 9.

San Francisco Chronicle, 1 May 1990, Six Star, p. 9.

Revenaugh, R.L. New Pride for an Old City Street. (1970, Mar 29). San Francisco Chronicle, p. 76.

San Francisco Chronicle, 29 Mar. 1970, Five Star FINAL Late Sports, p. 76.

Reza, H.G. Pipe Bomb Damages S.F. Women's Building. (1980, Oct 9). San Francisco Chronicle, p. 3.

San Francisco Chronicle, 9 Oct. 1980, Four Star, p. 3.

Rick ,Del Vecchio. Housing Project First For S.F. (1989, Jun 24). San Francisco Chronicle, p. 3.

San Francisco Chronicle, 24 Jun. 1989, Six Star, p. 3.

San Francisco Chronicle, 1 Aug. 1994, SPORTS FINAL, p. 1.

Roberts, Jerry. 14 Candidates in District 6 are Battling in Final Week. (1977, November 1). *San Francisco Chronicle*, p. 8.

Robertson, Michael. History of the Haight: It Was always a prime party place. (1987, April 9). *San Francisco Chronicle*, p. 26.

Schooling their Landlord (1974, Mar 7). San Francisco Chronicle, p. 7.

San Francisco Chronicle, 7 Mar. 1974, Four Star FINAL, p. 7.

Schwartz, Stephen. Noisy Protest: The Wrecking of Plaza West. (1989, Aug 18). San Francisco Chronicle, p. 2.

San Francisco Chronicle, 18 Aug. 1989, Six Star, p. 2.

Shilts, Randy. A Confrontation of Cultures. (1978, October 1). *San Francisco Chronicle*, p. 300.

S.F. Towers of Troubles. (1974, Mar 21). San Francisco Chronicle, p. 8.

San Francisco Chronicle, 21 Mar. 1974, Four Star FINAL, p. 8.

Silva, Elizabith Pepin, and Lewis Watts. *Harlem of the West.* Heydey Press, 2006.

Smith, Reginald. Tenants Defend their Housing (1983, Apr 12). San Francisco Chronicle, p. 4.

Some Gains at Geneva Towers (1974, Mar 26). San Francisco Chronicle, p. 28.

San Francisco Chronicle, 26 Mar. 1974, Four Star FINAL, p. 28.

Stewart, Pearl. Blast by Latino's Over Park Assault. (1980, Nov 14). San Francisco Chronicle, p. 21.

Starr, Kevin. Rebirth of a Neighborhood. (1989, Mar 26). San Francisco Chronicle, p. 350.

Suit Filed to Prevent Low Income Project (1988, Sep 8). San Francisco Chronicle, p. 24.

San Francisco Chronicle, 8 Sep. 1988, Six Star, p. 24.

Taylor Jr., Howard. A Question of a Squeeze on the Poor. January 27, 1986 (page 1 of 68). (1986, Jan 27).

Taylor Jr., Howard. S.F.'s black mecca passes into history. (1986, Jan 26). San Francisco Chronicle, p. 1.

San Francisco Chronicle, 26 Jan. 1986, Five Star, p. 1.

Taylor, Michael. Guilty Verdict in S.F. Gardener's Killing. (1977, December 9). *San Francisco Chronicle*, p. 29.

Temko, Allen. The New Market Street, an Unfulfilled Promise. (1979, Mar 21). San Francisco Chronicle, p. 4.

San Francisco Chronicle, 21 Mar. 1979, Four Star, p. 4.

Tonya Beasley: First Person. The New City. 1998, Apr 26). *San Francisco Chronicle*, p. 17.

San Francisco Chronicle, 26 Apr. 1998, SPORTS FINAL, p. 17.

Trager, Louis. Silicon Valley's sitting pretty: Market suddenly makes tech workers, stockholders rich. (1995, Jul 23). San Francisco Chronicle, p. 43.

San Francisco Chronicle, 23 Jul. 1995, SPORTS FINAL, p. 43.

Union Street Today A Triumph of Imagination. (1966, Jul 31). San Francisco Chronicle, p. 99.

San Francisco Chronicle, 31 Jul. 1966, FINAL Late Sports Four Star, p. 99.

Vecchio, Rick Del. S.F. Supervisors Remove Public Housing Obstacles. (1988, Jun 14). San Francisco Chronicle, p. 2.

San Francisco Chronicle, 14 Jun. 1988, Six Star, p. 2.

Vollmayer, Gloria. Trying to Save the Haight. (1972, May 2).

Walker, Thaai. Out From Under the Freeway: Gentrification a Mixed Blessing For Hayes Valley. (1993, Nov 2). San Francisco Chronicle, p. 1.

San Francisco Chronicle, 2 Nov. 1993, SPORTS FINAL, p. 1.

Walker, T. (1993, Nov 2). Some Tenants Won't Get to Come Back - Tearing down blighted housing will push out 170 low-income families. *THE SAN FRANCISCO CHRONICLE*, p. A6.

About the Author

Originally from Milwaukee, Wisconsin, Lorenzo Gomez is a graduate of the University of San Francisco and the Rossier School of Education. He writes on issues of contemporary American history.

Made in the USA
Middletown, DE
10 April 2022